JUMBLE® Neighbor

Puzzles that Bring People Together!

Henri Arnold,
Bob Lee,
Jeff Knurek, &
David L. Hoyt

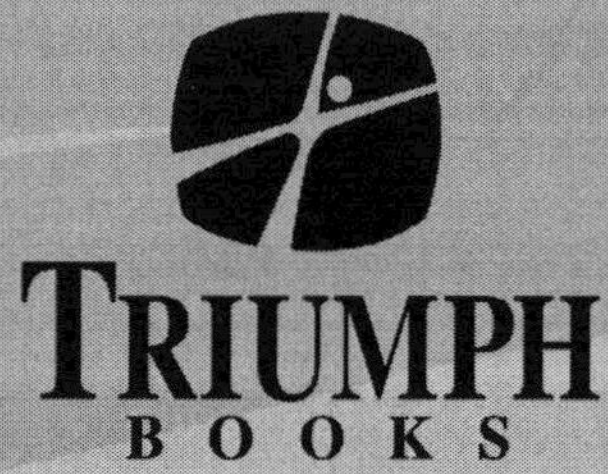

TRIUMPH
BOOKS

This book is available in quantity at special discounts
for your group or organization.

For further information, contact:
Triumph Books LLC
814 North Franklin Street
Chicago, Illinois 60610
Phone: (312) 337-0747
www.triumphbooks.com

Printed in U.S.A.

ISBN: 978-1-62937-845-9

Design by Sue Knopf

Contents

JUMBLE® Neighbor

Classic Puzzles

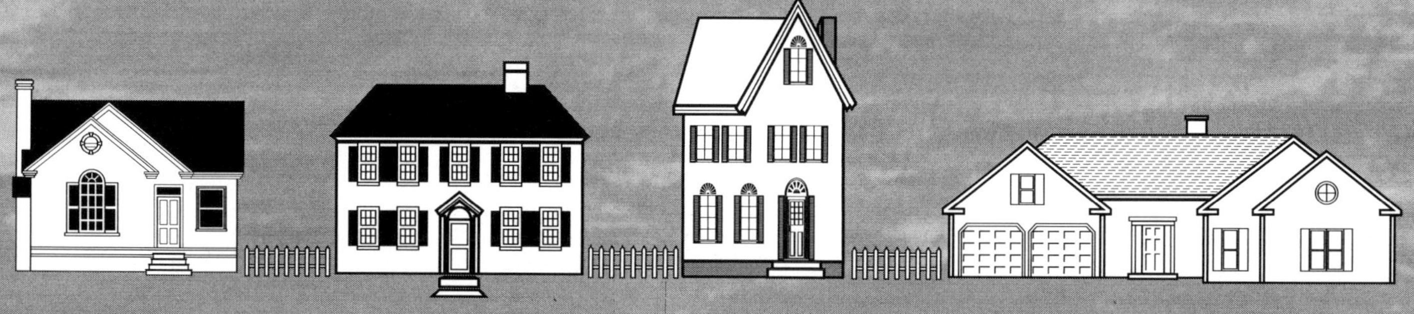

JUMBLE®

Unscramble these four Jumbles, one letter to each square, to form four ordinary words.

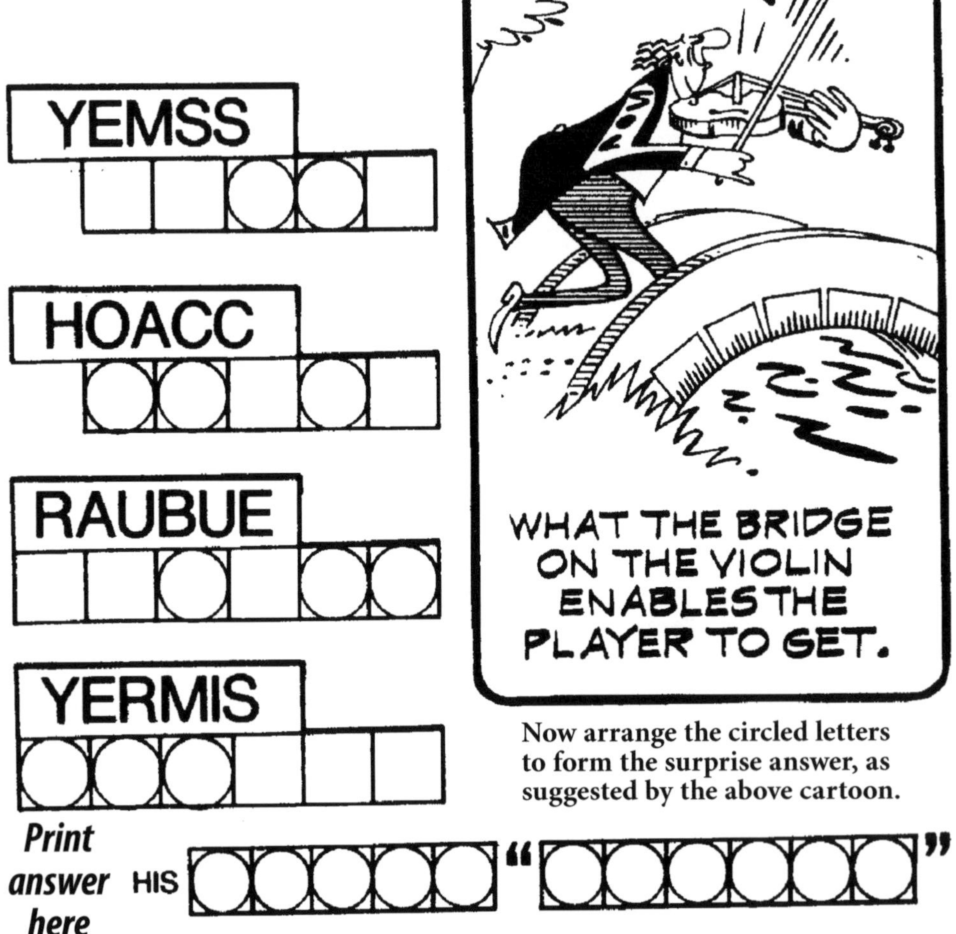
YEMSS
HOACC
RAUBUE
YERMIS
WHAT THE BRIDGE ON THE VIOLIN ENABLES THE PLAYER TO GET.
Print answer here
HIS

Now arrange the circled letters to form the surprise answer, as suggested by the above cartoon.

JUMBLE®

Unscramble these four Jumbles, one letter to each square, to form four ordinary words.

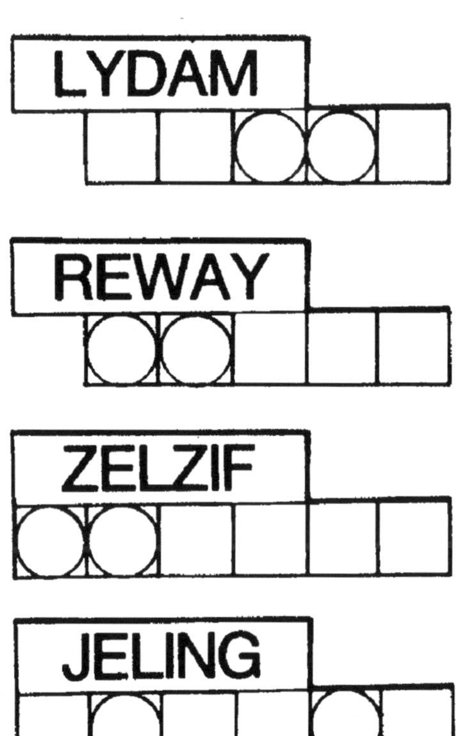
LYDAM
REWAY
ZELZIF
JELING

FORMERLY FOUND ONLY IN THE COUNTRY BUT NOW COMMONLY SEEN IN THE CITY.

Now arrange the circled letters to form the surprise answer, as suggested by the above cartoon.

Print answer here

JUMBLE®

Unscramble these four Jumbles, one letter to each square, to form four ordinary words.

TALNS
MANUH
INLOVI
FLUWOE
He won't talk to anyone
WHAT THE BIGAMIST WOULD LIKE TO KEEP.

Now arrange the circled letters to form the surprise answer, as suggested by the above cartoon.

Print answer here

JUMBLE®

Unscramble these four Jumbles, one letter to each square, to form four ordinary words.

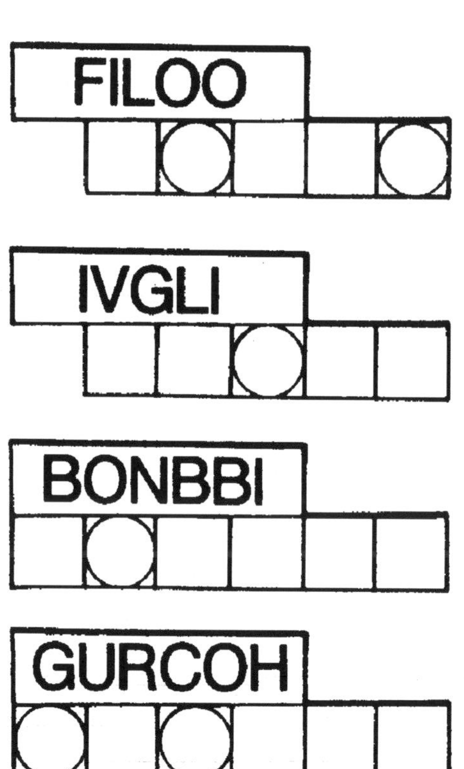
FILOO
IVGLI
BONBBI
GURCOH

WHAT WERE ALEXANDER GRAHAM BELL'S FIRST WORDS?

Now arrange the circled letters to form the surprise answer, as suggested by the above cartoon.

Print answer here 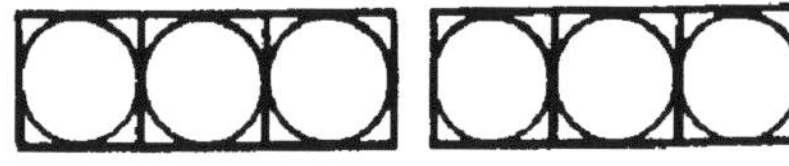

JUMBLE®

Unscramble these four Jumbles, one letter to each square, to form four ordinary words.

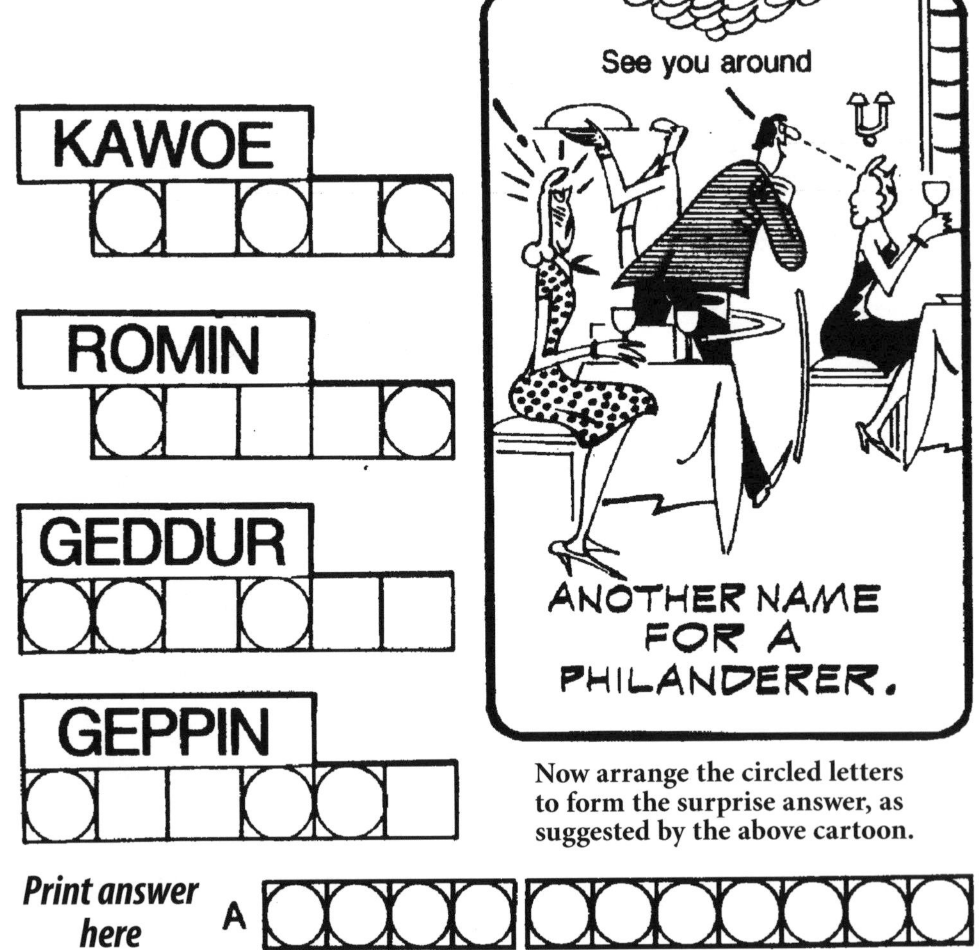
KAWOE
ROMIN
GEDDUR
GEPPIN
See you around
ANOTHER NAME FOR A PHILANDERER.
Print answer here
A

Now arrange the circled letters to form the surprise answer, as suggested by the above cartoon.

JUMBLE®

Unscramble these four Jumbles, one letter to each square, to form four ordinary words.

GEWED
NARBD
YIKELL
REWEPT
Can't find a thing wrong with you
You're not trying!
WHAT THE HYPOCHONDRIAC WAS SICK OF.

Now arrange the circled letters to form the surprise answer, as suggested by the above cartoon.

Print answer here

JUMBLE®

Unscramble these four Jumbles, one letter to each square, to form four ordinary words.

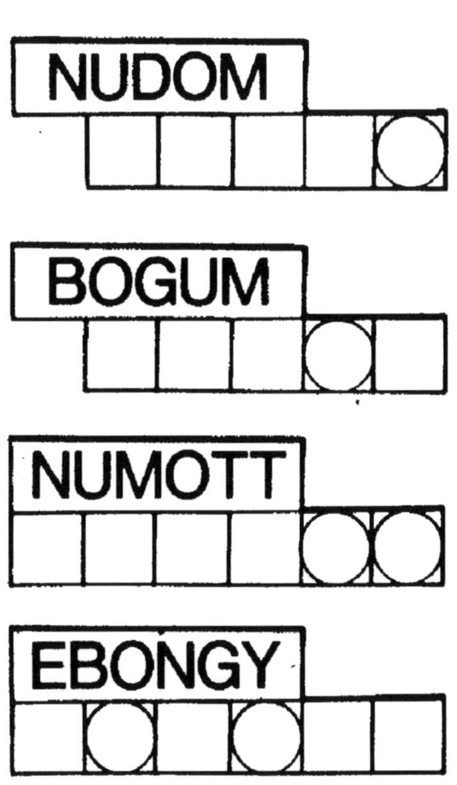
NUDOM
BOGUM
NUMOTT
EBONGY

You're always right, J.B.!
WHAT SOMEBODY WHO TRIES TO PLEASE EVERYBODY IS APT TO REMAIN.

Now arrange the circled letters to form the surprise answer, as suggested by the above cartoon.

Print answer here A 

JUMBLE®

Unscramble these four Jumbles, one letter to each square, to form four ordinary words.

GARBE
YALFE
NATTYR
HOLURY
WHAT THEY CALLED HER HUSBAND WHO WAS ADDICTED TO GAMBLING.

Now arrange the circled letters to form the surprise answer, as suggested by the above cartoon.

Print answer here HER " "

JUMBLE®

Unscramble these four Jumbles, one letter to each square, to form four ordinary words.

FLECT
UGIED
KONYED
LANFEX
A DAY OFF IS SOMETIMES FOLLOWED BY THIS.

Now arrange the circled letters to form the surprise answer, as suggested by the above cartoon.

Print answer here AN

JUMBLE®

Unscramble these four Jumbles, one letter to each square, to form four ordinary words.

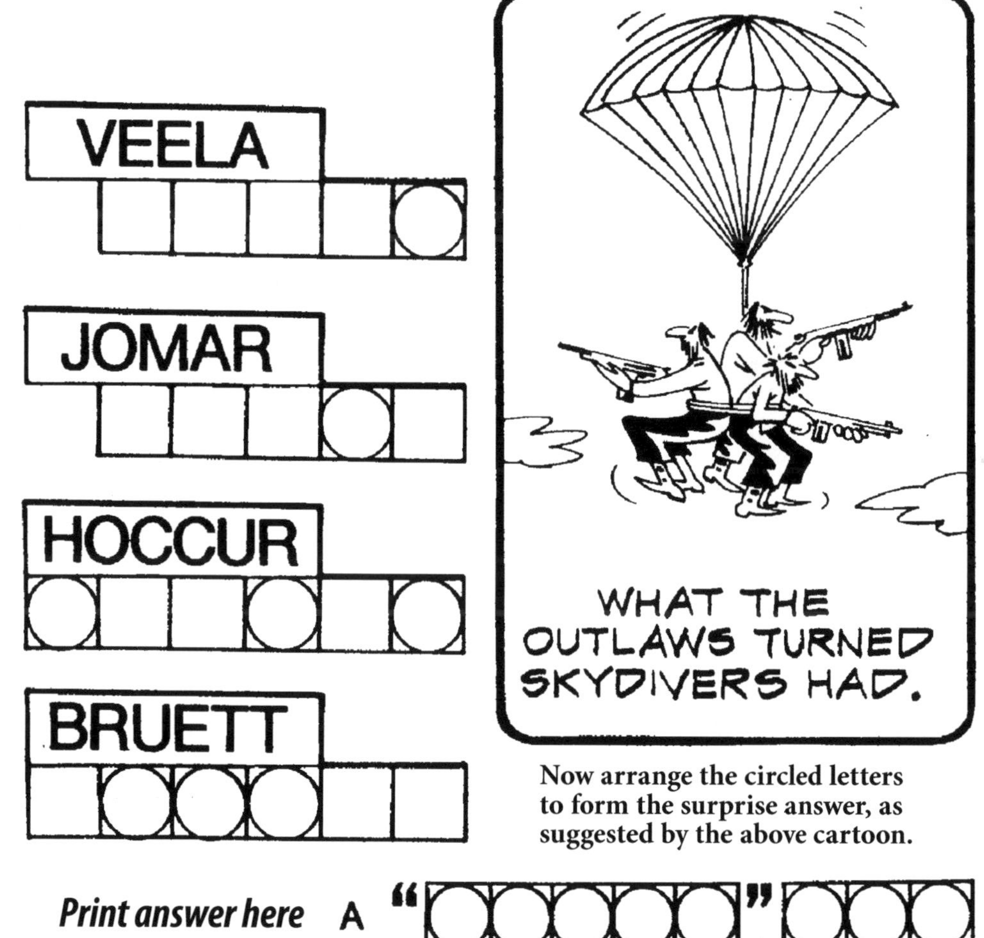
VEELA
JOMAR
HOCCUR
BRUETT
WHAT THE OUTLAWS TURNED SKYDIVERS HAD.

Now arrange the circled letters to form the surprise answer, as suggested by the above cartoon.

Print answer here A "◯◯◯◯◯" ◯◯◯

JUMBLE®

Unscramble these four Jumbles, one letter to each square, to form four ordinary words.

IXOCT

CATHY

GRUHNY

WURCEF

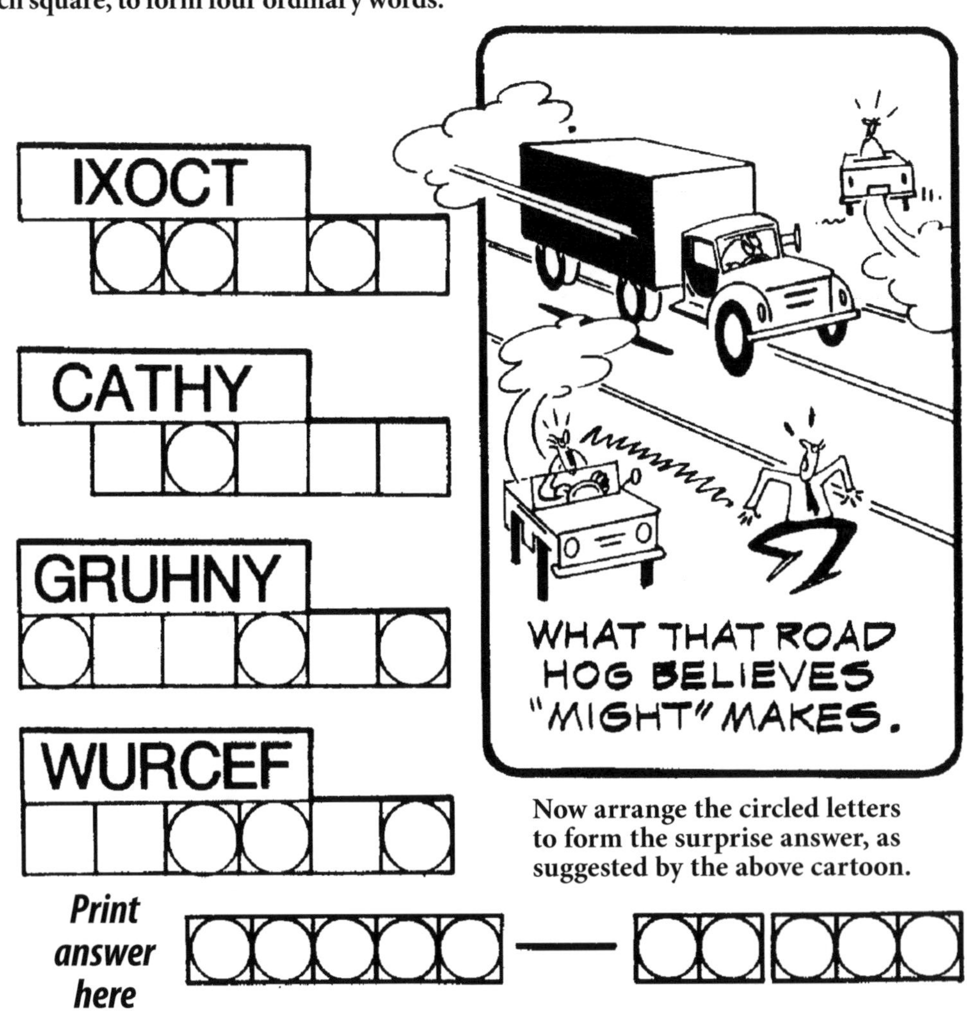
WHAT THAT ROAD HOG BELIEVES "MIGHT" MAKES.

Now arrange the circled letters to form the surprise answer, as suggested by the above cartoon.

Print answer here

JUMBLE®

Unscramble these four Jumbles, one letter to each square, to form four ordinary words.

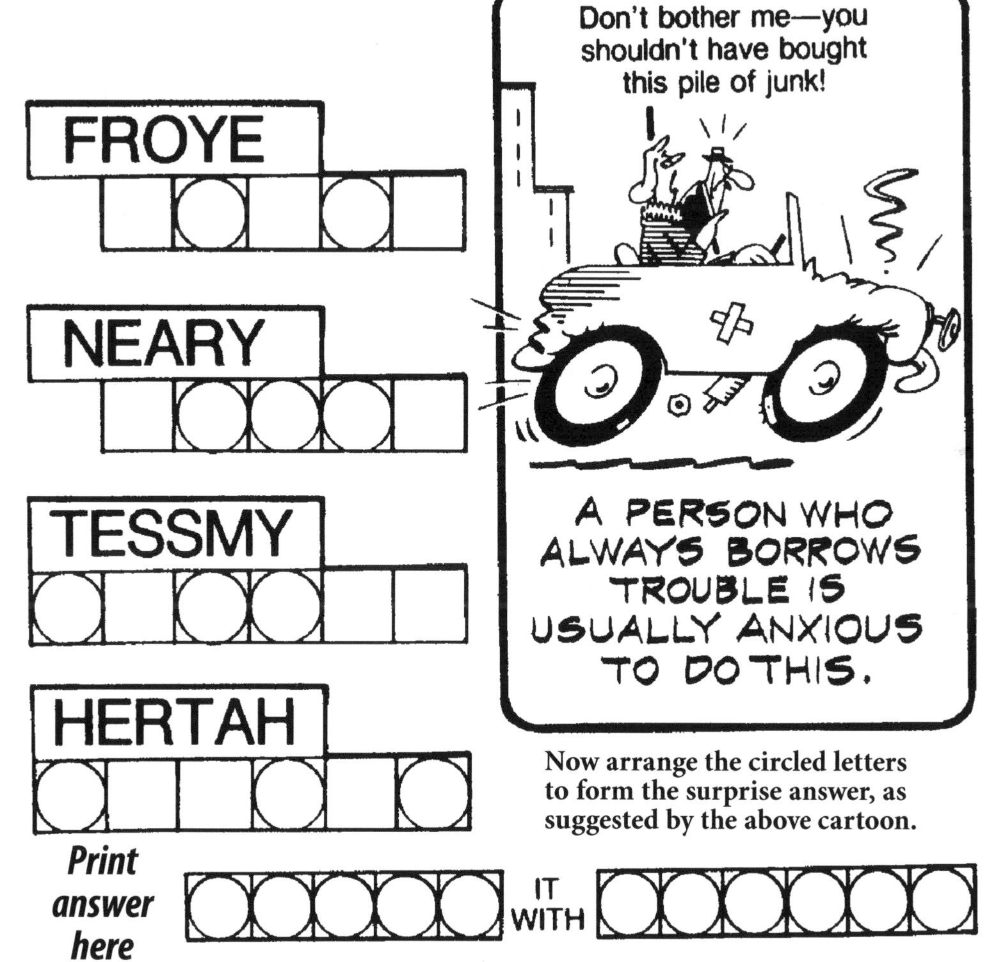
FROYE
NEARY
TESSMY
HERTAH
Don't bother me—you shouldn't have bought this pile of junk!
A PERSON WHO ALWAYS BORROWS TROUBLE IS USUALLY ANXIOUS TO DO THIS.

Now arrange the circled letters to form the surprise answer, as suggested by the above cartoon.

Print answer here ◯◯◯◯◯ IT WITH ◯◯◯◯◯◯

JUMBLE®

Unscramble these four Jumbles, one letter to each square, to form four ordinary words.

ROMUN
RUTTE
FOYFAL
DEWPOR
WHAT YEAST IS.
Now arrange the circled letters to form the surprise answer, as suggested by the above cartoon.
Print answer here

JUMBLE®

Unscramble these four Jumbles, one letter to each square, to form four ordinary words.

AGELL

TIARE

DARNBY

TARIBB

Now that we're so rich, you'll have time to fix the fence one of these days
ANOTHER NAME FOR SARCASM.

Now arrange the circled letters to form the surprise answer, as suggested by the above cartoon.

Print answer here ______ "___"

JUMBLE®

Unscramble these four Jumbles, one letter to each square, to form four ordinary words.

NOMEW
DOIMI
THOTEG
STOJEL
HE LIES IN WAIT FOR A FISH, AND AFTER CATCHING IT HE DOES THIS.
Now arrange the circled letters to form the surprise answer, as suggested by the above cartoon.
Print answer here
IN

JUMBLE®

Unscramble these four Jumbles, one letter to each square, to form four ordinary words.

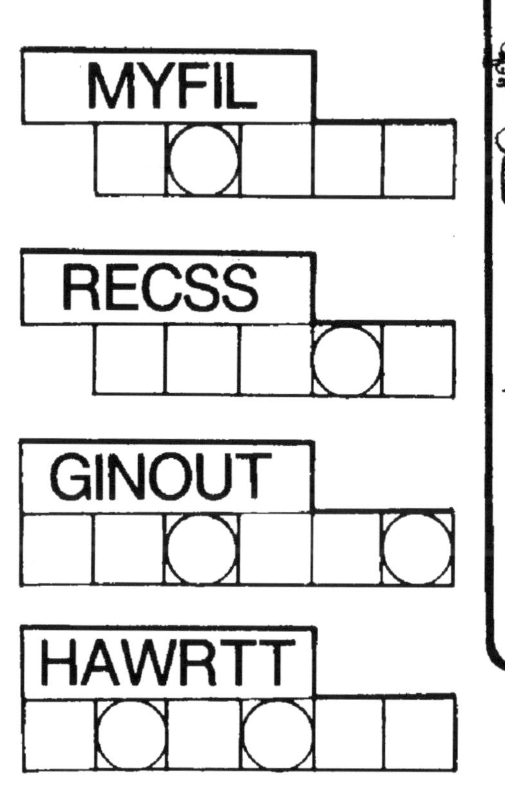
MYFIL
RECSS
GINOUT
HAWRTT

ON A BLIND DATE HE WAS EXPECTING A "VISION," BUT IT TURNED OUT TO BE THIS.

Now arrange the circled letters to form the surprise answer, as suggested by the above cartoon.

Print answer here

JUMBLE®

Unscramble these four Jumbles, one letter to each square, to form four ordinary words.

TEYIP

WARFE

FORLEG

VITHER

WHAT THE BUS DRIVER TOLD HIM.

Now arrange the circled letters to form the surprise answer, as suggested by the above cartoon.

Print answer here TO

JUMBLE®

Unscramble these four Jumbles, one letter to each square, to form four ordinary words.

Every time he opens his mouth he reveals his ignorance
ONE WAY TO SAVE FACE IS TO LEARN TO KEEP THIS.

THRIM

CITHY

WURPAD

RASHEE

Now arrange the circled letters to form the surprise answer, as suggested by the above cartoon.

Print answer here ☐☐☐☐ OF IT ☐☐☐☐

JUMBLE®

Unscramble these four Jumbles, one letter to each square, to form four ordinary words.

BREYD
TOJUS
SAKMAD
NELPOL
I guess he has no more time for me
A WOMAN CAN SAY MORE IN A LOOK THAN A MAN CAN IN THIS.

Now arrange the circled letters to form the surprise answer, as suggested by the above cartoon.

Print answer here

JUMBLE®

Unscramble these four Jumbles, one letter to each square, to form four ordinary words.

TIGAN
RAMOA
SHORUC
TULIED
I can't see myself getting rich here. Think I'll quit
IF A JOB IS TO HAVE A FUTURE, IT'S LIKELY TO DEPEND ON THIS.

Now arrange the circled letters to form the surprise answer, as suggested by the above cartoon.

Print answer here THE ( ) ( ) ( ) WHO ( ) ( ) ( ) ( ) ( ) ( ) ( )

PUZZLE 21

JUMBLE®

Unscramble these four Jumbles, one letter to each square, to form four ordinary words.

TIFAN
POOTH
GERDED
TYSSUL
A GUY WHO'S ALWAYS BOASTING ABOUT HIS FAMILY TREE PROBABLY COMES FROM THIS.

Now arrange the circled letters to form the surprise answer, as suggested by the above cartoon.

Print answer here ITS

JUMBLE®

Unscramble these four Jumbles, one letter to each square, to form four ordinary words.

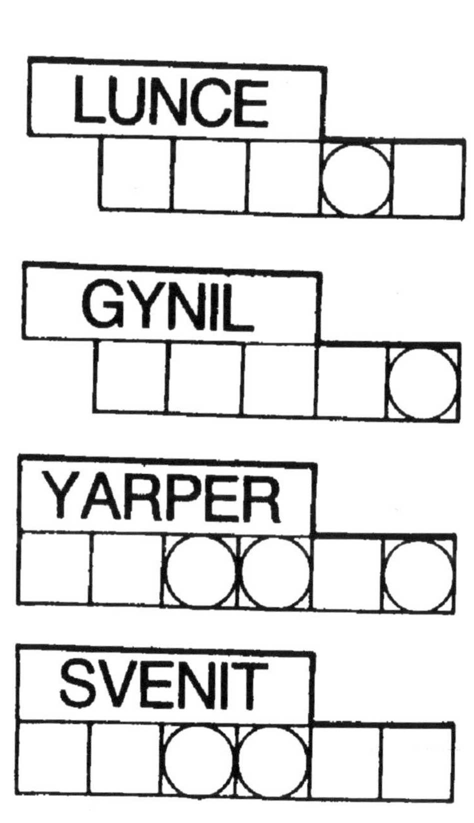
LUNCE
GYNIL
YARPER
SVENIT

$
WILL
HOW THE UNDERTAKER PRESENTED HIS BILL.

Now arrange the circled letters to form the surprise answer, as suggested by the above cartoon.

Print answer here 

JUMBLE®

Unscramble these four Jumbles, one letter to each square, to form four ordinary words.

MAFER
THICH
UNCOBE
BUESAD
Looks gorgeous on you!
$7,000
$7,000
$8,000
$5,000
SHE HAS WHAT IT TAKES TO WEAR THE LATEST FASHIONS—

Now arrange the circled letters to form the surprise answer, as suggested by the above cartoon.

Print answer here A

JUMBLE®

Unscramble these four Jumbles, one letter to each square, to form four ordinary words.

NEETA
FECEN
DRIHNE
INDATE
GOLIATH WAS SURPRISED BY WHAT DAVID DID BECAUSE SUCH A THING HAD NEVER THIS BEFORE.

Now arrange the circled letters to form the surprise answer, as suggested by the above cartoon.

Print answer here ○○○○○○○ HIS ○○○○

JUMBLE®

Unscramble these four Jumbles, one letter to each square, to form four ordinary words.

VABER
WOYLL
FADGYL
NURTHE
THAT WINDBAG WAS ALWAYS GETTING CARRIED AWAY BY THE SOUND OF HIS OWN VOICE, BUT NEVER THIS.

Now arrange the circled letters to form the surprise answer, as suggested by the above cartoon.

Print answer here

JUMBLE®

Neighbor

Daily Puzzles

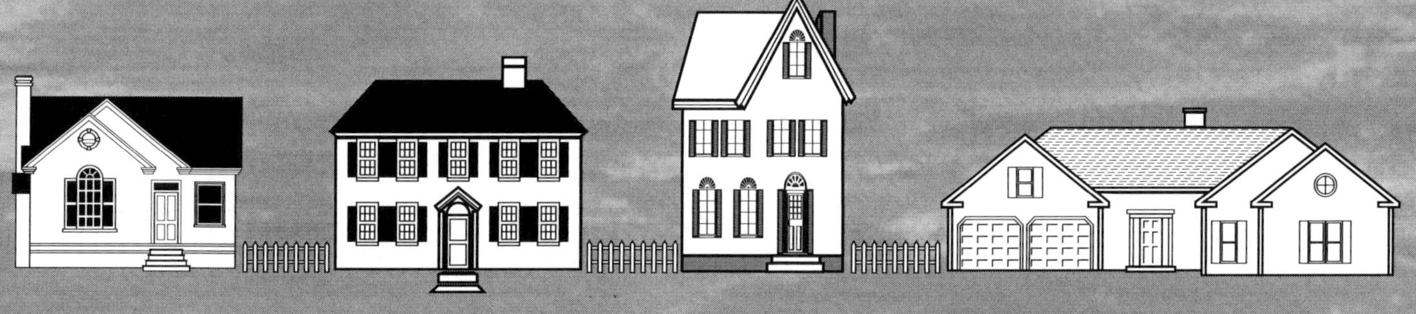

JUMBLE®

Unscramble these four Jumbles, one letter to each square, to form four ordinary words.

HOTOT
PECOU
LIKLER
LANDAV
SHE WAS NEVER OVERLOOKED, BUT USUALLY THIS.

Now arrange the circled letters to form the surprise answer, as suggested by the above cartoon.

Print answer here

JUMBLE®

Unscramble these four Jumbles, one letter to each square, to form four ordinary words.

KANOE
GREME
LASTOP
ENMURB
I knew it all along
A PERSON WHO WAKES UP TO FIND HIMSELF FAMOUS MAY NOT HAVE THIS.

Now arrange the circled letters to form the surprise answer, as suggested by the above cartoon.

Print answer here

JUMBLE®

Unscramble these four Jumbles, one letter to each square, to form four ordinary words.

TCHAB
KORJE
DILQUI
UPVERY
WHEN THE KIDS HAVE TO PLAY IN ON ACCOUNT OF OF BAD WEATHER, THE PARENTS OFTEN END UP THIS WAY.

Now arrange the circled letters to form the surprise answer, as suggested by the above cartoon.

Print answer here

JUMBLE®

Unscramble these four Jumbles, one letter to each square, to form four ordinary words.

DRAUF
POATI
PENMAD
ECOLLA
How about a drink?
Just a wee one
THAT VISITOR WHO DROPS IN FOR A CALL MIGHT ACTUALLY BE WANTING TO DO THIS.

Now arrange the circled letters to form the surprise answer, as suggested by the above cartoon.

Print answer here FOR A

JUMBLE®

Unscramble these four Jumbles, one letter to each square, to form four ordinary words.

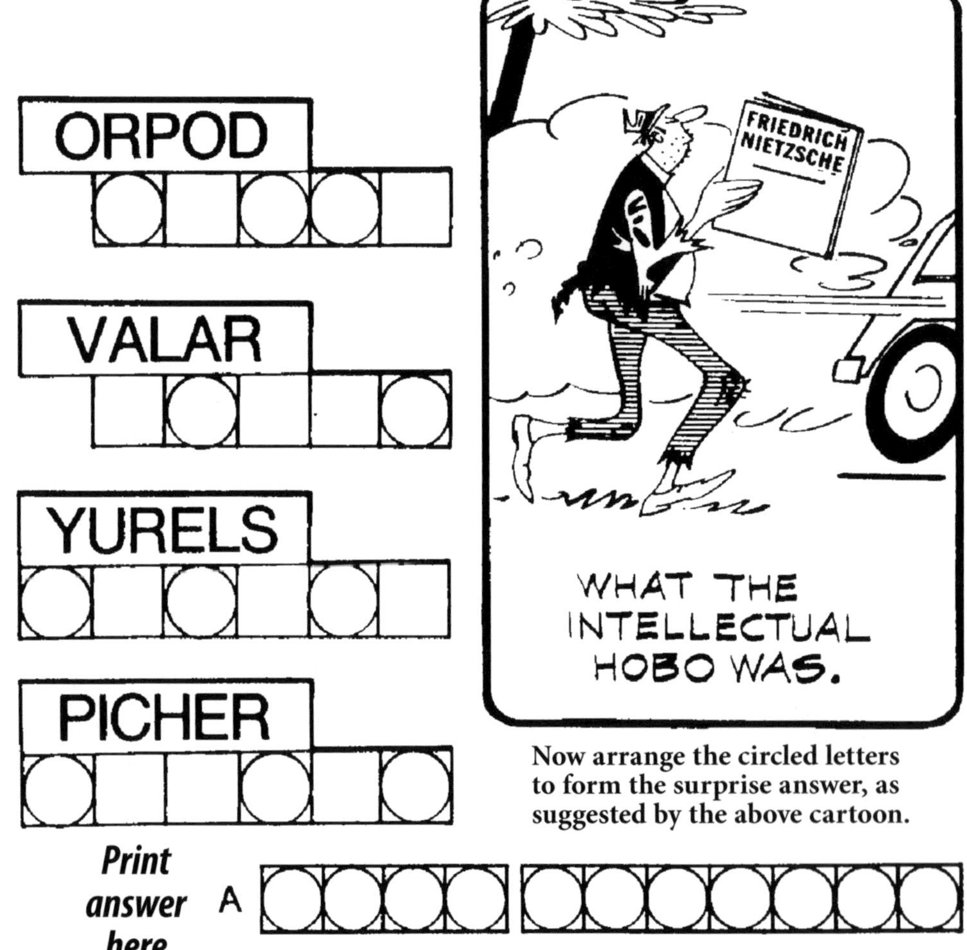
ORPOD
VALAR
YURELS
PICHER
FRIEDRICH NIETZSCHE
WHAT THE INTELLECTUAL HOBO WAS.
Now arrange the circled letters to form the surprise answer, as suggested by the above cartoon.
Print answer here
A

JUMBLE®

Unscramble these four Jumbles, one letter to each square, to form four ordinary words.

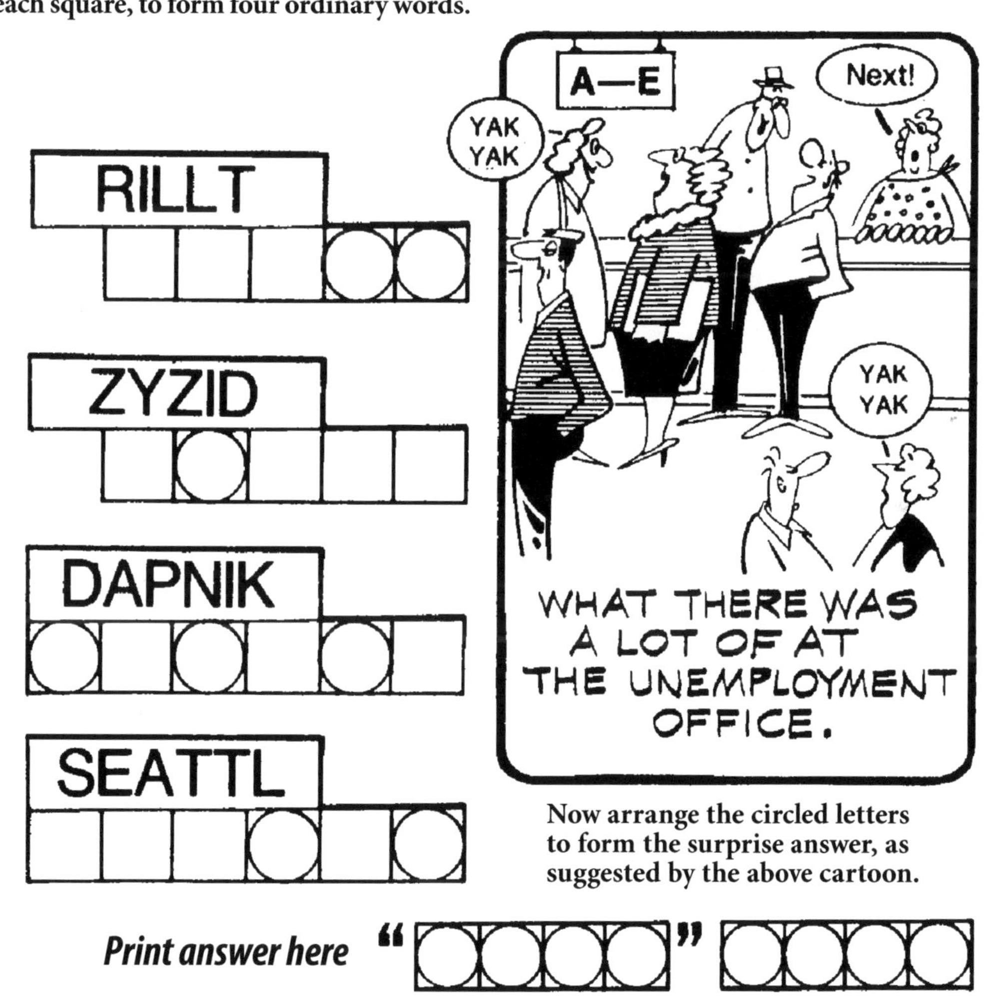
RILLT
ZYZID
DAPNIK
SEATTL
A—E
Next!
YAK YAK
YAK YAK
WHAT THERE WAS A LOT OF AT THE UNEMPLOYMENT OFFICE.

Now arrange the circled letters to form the surprise answer, as suggested by the above cartoon.

Print answer here " ◯◯◯◯ " ◯◯◯◯

JUMBLE®

Unscramble these four Jumbles, one letter to each square, to form four ordinary words.

AKQUE

DRATY

LESCUM

DAGAPO

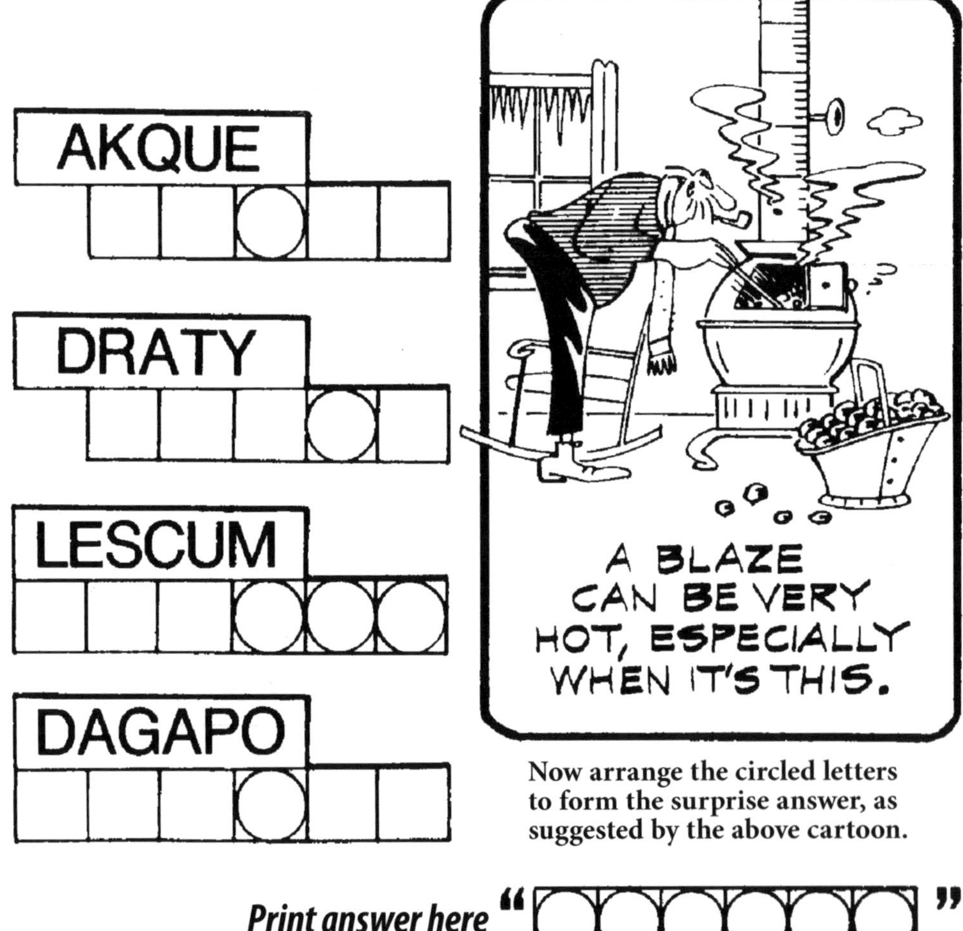
A BLAZE CAN BE VERY HOT, ESPECIALLY WHEN IT'S THIS.

Now arrange the circled letters to form the surprise answer, as suggested by the above cartoon.

Print answer here " ○○○○○○ "

JUMBLE®

Unscramble these four Jumbles, one letter to each square, to form four ordinary words.

ENMOY
USSOE
RIVLIE
MUPTIE
No hot water
No heat
Needs painting
THE LANDLORD'S PROMISES WERE NO BETTER THAN THIS.

Now arrange the circled letters to form the surprise answer, as suggested by the above cartoon.

Print answer here HIS

JUMBLE®

Unscramble these four Jumbles, one letter to each square, to form four ordinary words.

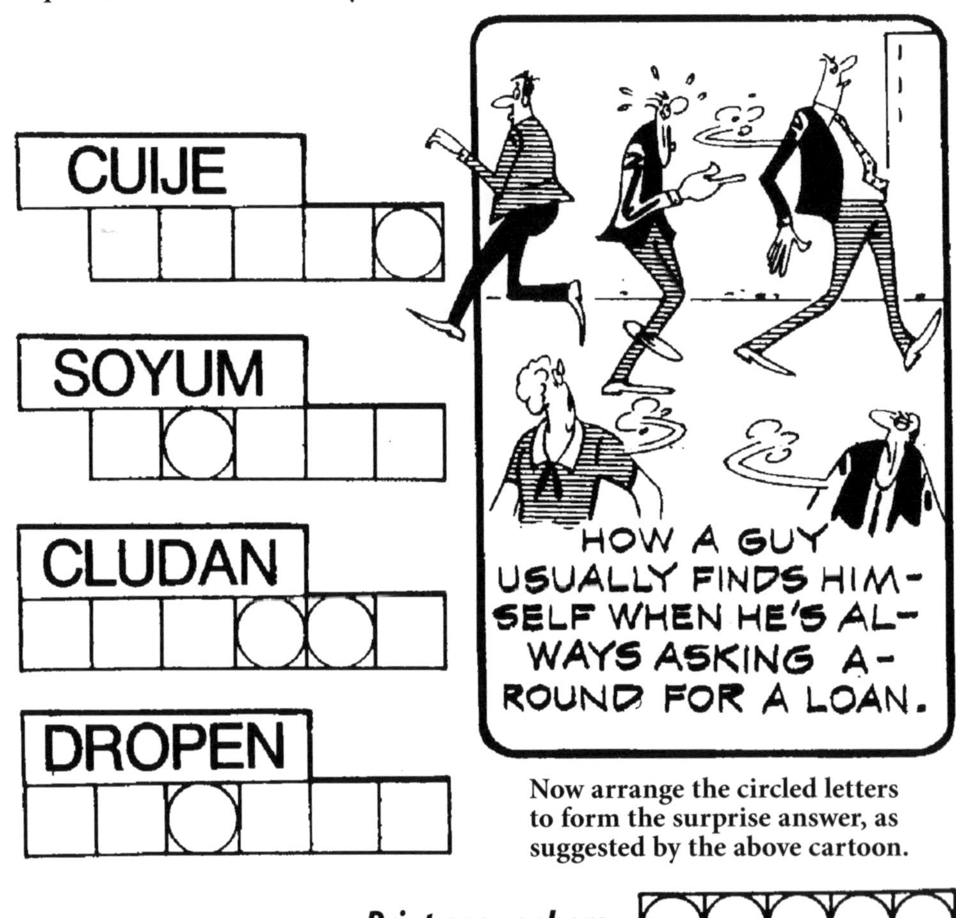
CUIJE
SOYUM
CLUDAN
DROPEN
HOW A GUY USUALLY FINDS HIM- SELF WHEN HE'S AL- WAYS ASKING A- ROUND FOR A LOAN.

Now arrange the circled letters to form the surprise answer, as suggested by the above cartoon.

Print answer here

JUMBLE®

Unscramble these four Jumbles, one letter to each square, to form four ordinary words.

OPYPP
RIPEV
NOPETT
GLAJEN
I can recall everything
WHAT A GOOD MEMORY REQUIRES.

Now arrange the circled letters to form the surprise answer, as suggested by the above cartoon.

Print answer here OR

JUMBLE®

Unscramble these four Jumbles, one letter to each square, to form four ordinary words.

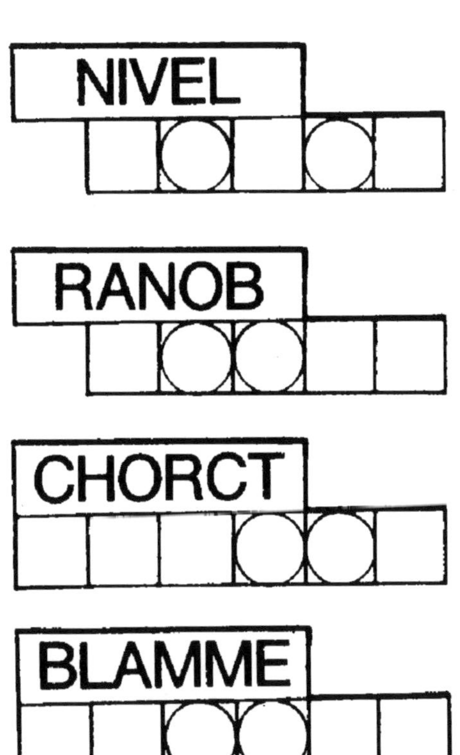
NIVEL
RANOB
CHORCT
BLAMME

I wouldn't be caught dead in that filthy place
WHAT THEY CALLED THE REAR ENTRANCE OF THAT CAFETERIA.

Now arrange the circled letters to form the surprise answer, as suggested by the above cartoon.

Print answer here THE 

JUMBLE®

Unscramble these four Jumbles, one letter to each square, to form four ordinary words.

MOUDI
NAPAD
WERKES
NORGAD
HOW THEY FELT WHEN TEACHER GAVE A ZERO TO EVERYONE IN THE CLASS.
Now arrange the circled letters to form the surprise answer, as suggested by the above cartoon.
Print answer here
" - "

JUMBLE®

Unscramble these four Jumbles, one letter to each square, to form four ordinary words.

PIRAD
VEREF
KOOPHU
ARTUNI
WHAT THE
LOAFER'S LIFE
WORK WAS.

Now arrange the circled letters to form the surprise answer, as suggested by the above cartoon.

Print answer here ☐☐ ☐☐☐☐☐ IT

JUMBLE®

Unscramble these four Jumbles, one letter to each square, to form four ordinary words.

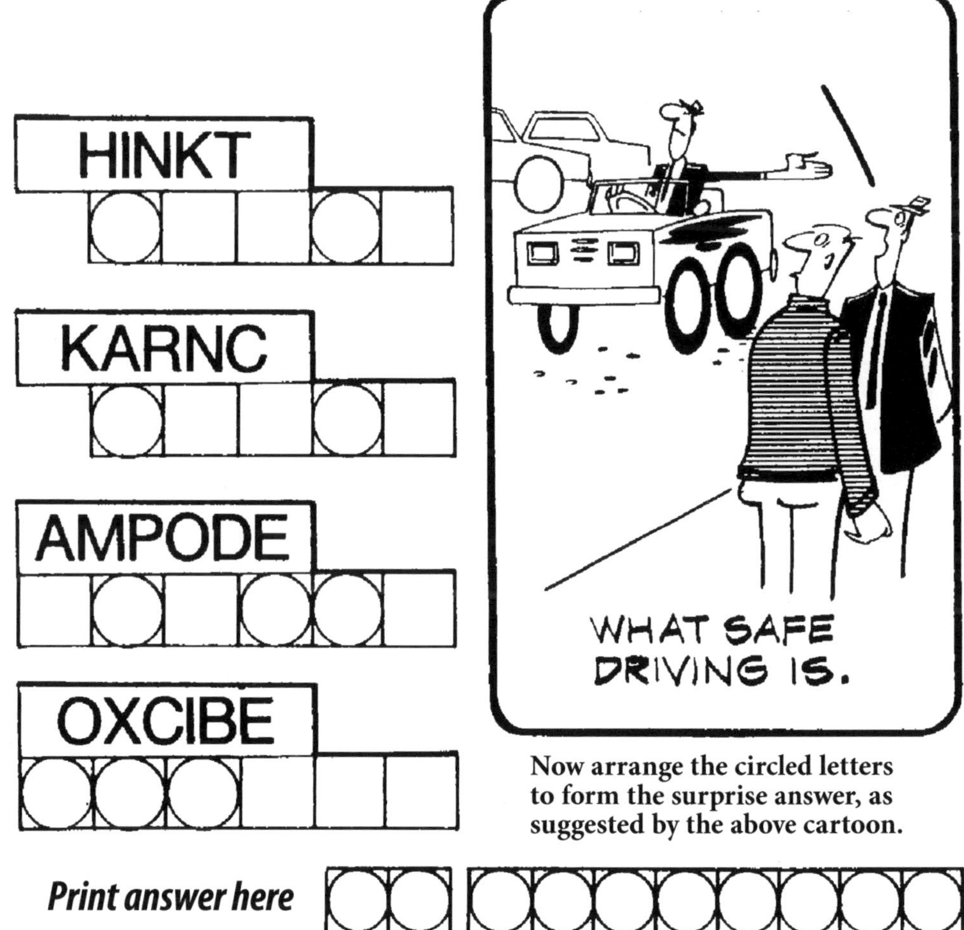
HINKT
KARNC
AMPODE
OXCIBE
WHAT SAFE DRIVING IS.

Now arrange the circled letters to form the surprise answer, as suggested by the above cartoon.

Print answer here

JUMBLE®

Unscramble these four Jumbles, one letter to each square, to form four ordinary words.

VASUE
WADAR
BLUMJE
NUCKOL
FOR AN OPINION TO BE SOUND IT MUST NOT BE THIS.

Now arrange the circled letters to form the surprise answer, as suggested by the above cartoon.

Print answer here

JUMBLE®

Unscramble these four Jumbles, one letter to each square, to form four ordinary words.

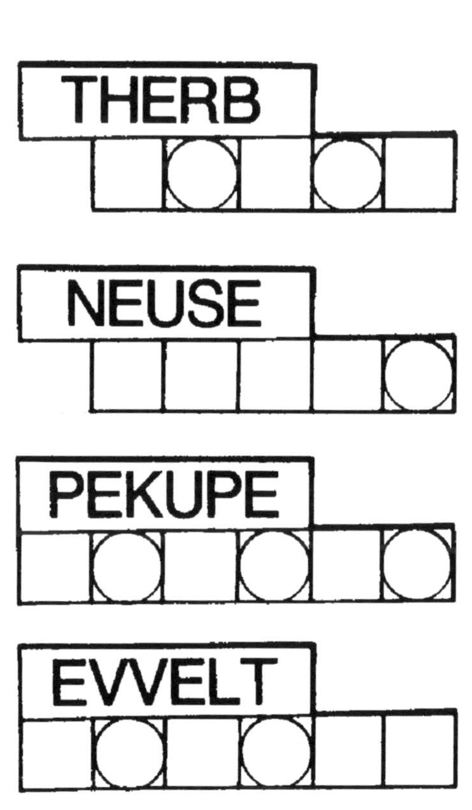
THERB
NEUSE
PEKUPE
EVVELT

WHAT HIS WIFE'S LITTLE POODLE WAS.

Now arrange the circled letters to form the surprise answer, as suggested by the above cartoon.

Print answer here HIS

JUMBLE®

Unscramble these four Jumbles, one letter to each square, to form four ordinary words.

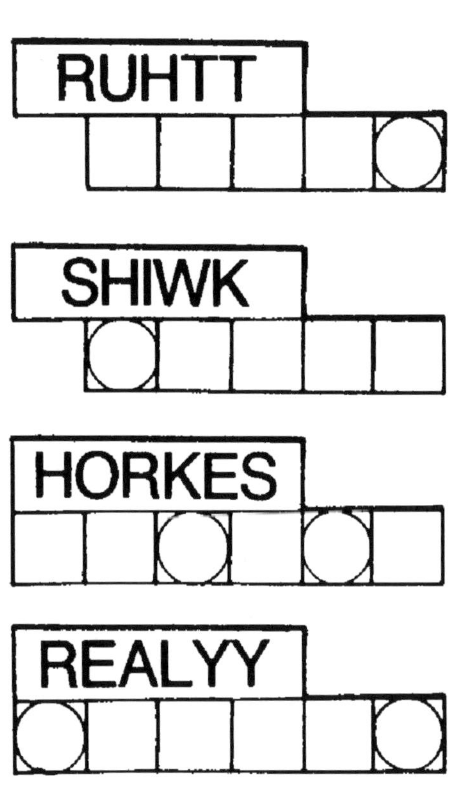
RUHTT
SHIWK
HORKES
REALYY

WHAT THE "WINO" SAID WHEN OFFERED A LITTLE SIP.

Now arrange the circled letters to form the surprise answer, as suggested by the above cartoon.

Print answer here “, ”

JUMBLE®

Unscramble these four Jumbles, one letter to each square, to form four ordinary words.

PHRAC
HILEW
TINKTE
CHIPUC
WHAT A MARRIAGE PROPOSAL IS.
Now arrange the circled letters to form the surprise answer, as suggested by the above cartoon.
Print answer here
A

JUMBLE®

Unscramble these four Jumbles, one letter to each square, to form four ordinary words.

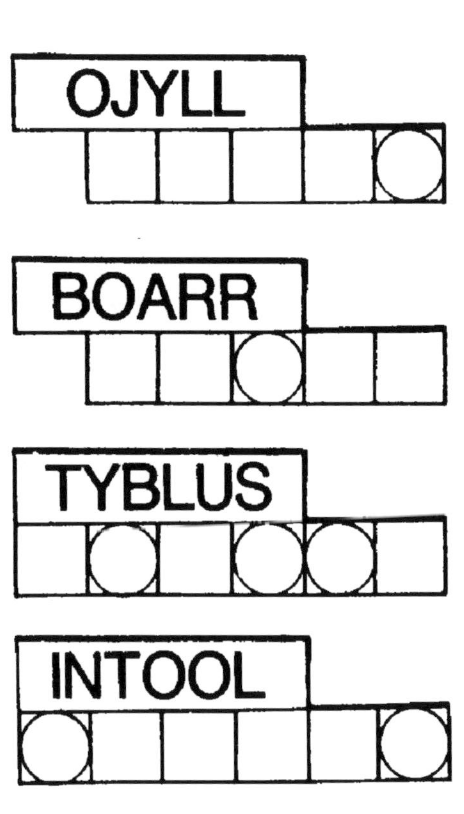
OJYLL
BOARR
TYBLUS
INTOOL

HOW "SHARP" REMARKS MAY BE EXPRESSED, ODDLY ENOUGH.

Now arrange the circled letters to form the surprise answer, as suggested by the above cartoon.

Print answer here 

JUMBLE®

Unscramble these four Jumbles, one letter to each square, to form four ordinary words.

HOCKE

TRAYP

RUFUTE

DIMPIL

Regarding the economy . . .
AMERICA'S MOST OUTSTANDING PUBLIC FIGURE.

Now arrange the circled letters to form the surprise answer, as suggested by the above cartoon.

Print answer here

JUMBLE®

Unscramble these four Jumbles, one letter to each square, to form four ordinary words.

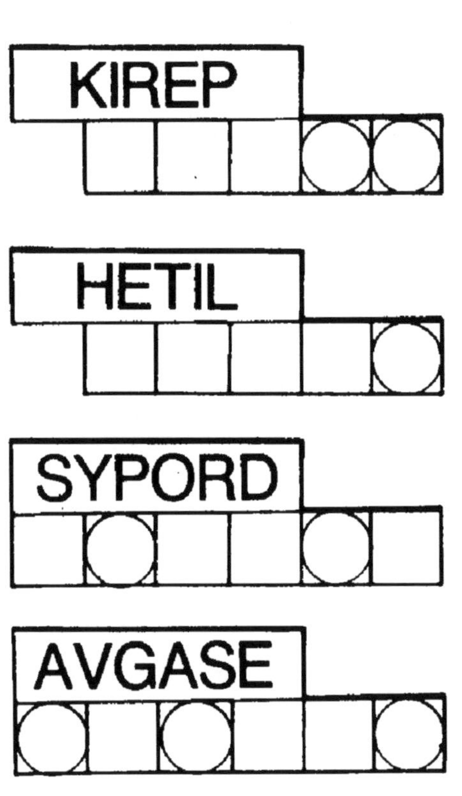
KIREP
HETIL
SYPORD
AVGASE

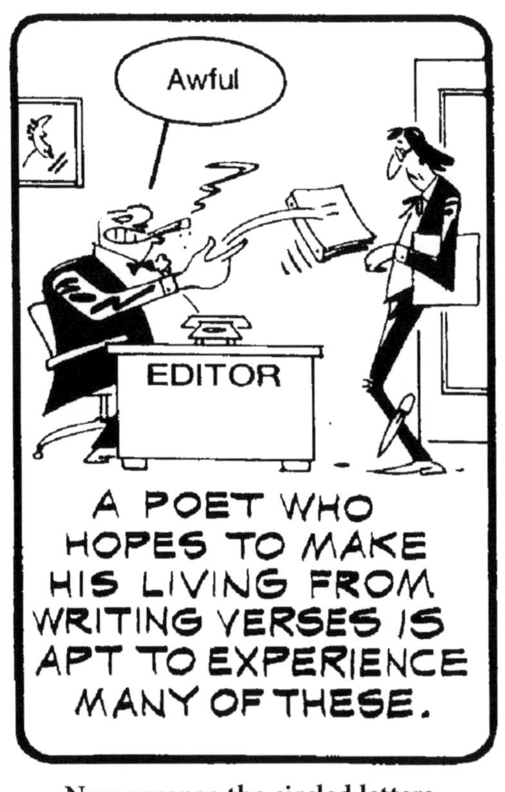
Awful
EDITOR
A POET WHO HOPES TO MAKE HIS LIVING FROM WRITING VERSES IS APT TO EXPERIENCE MANY OF THESE.

Now arrange the circled letters to form the surprise answer, as suggested by the above cartoon.

Print answer here

JUMBLE®

Unscramble these four Jumbles, one letter to each square, to form four ordinary words.

WATEK
GEEBI
DOMBEY
SCAFAR
WHY THOSE OTHER DOCTORS RESENTED THE ORTHOPEDIST.
Now arrange the circled letters to form the surprise answer, as suggested by the above cartoon.
Print answer here
HE
ALL THE

JUMBLE®

Unscramble these four Jumbles, one letter to each square, to form four ordinary words.

UNGED
LINTE
GASYRS
DEPLUH
E=mc²
A NUCLEAR PHYSICIST IS ANOTHER MAN WHOSE WIFE DOESN'T THIS.

Now arrange the circled letters to form the surprise answer, as suggested by the above cartoon.

Print answer here HIM

JUMBLE®

Unscramble these four Jumbles, one letter to each square, to form four ordinary words.

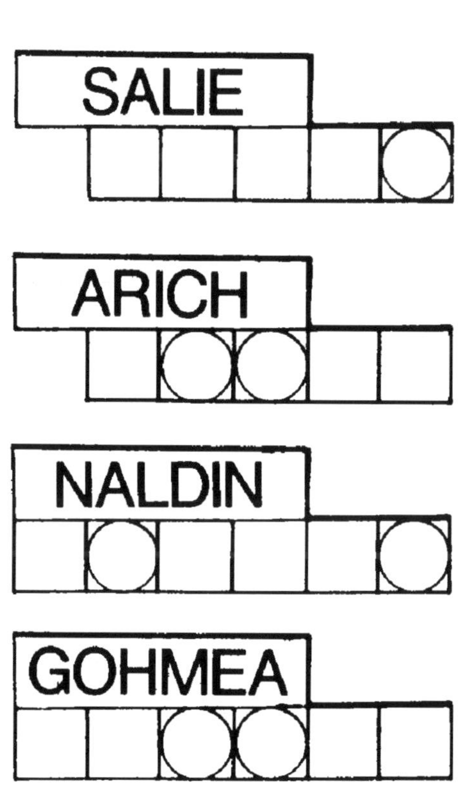
SALIE
ARICH
NALDIN
GOHMEA

Sounds like skullduggery to me
WHAT THE PHRENOLOGIST WAS.

Now arrange the circled letters to form the surprise answer, as suggested by the above cartoon.

Print answer here

JUMBLE®

Unscramble these four Jumbles, one letter to each square, to form four ordinary words.

GOINJ
HAFES
FLIPER
SUMMUE
WHAT THE HEROIC FIREMAN BECAME.

Now arrange the circled letters to form the surprise answer, as suggested by the above cartoon.

Print answer here " ◯◯◯◯-◯◯◯ "

JUMBLE®

Unscramble these four Jumbles, one letter to each square, to form four ordinary words.

PYMUB
GLOUM
WECHEN
NALLEF
Go all the way!
WHAT THEY THOUGHT WHEN HE ROUNDED SECOND BASE.
Now arrange the circled letters to form the surprise answer, as suggested by the above cartoon.
Print answer here
THERE'S NO
LIKE

JUMBLE®

Unscramble these four Jumbles, one letter to each square, to form four ordinary words.

KETOS
TIFED
DRAFTI
OSMACT
Makes my mouth water
RESTAURANT
Yum yum
PEOPLE WHO LOVE SHELLFISH BECOME HUNGRY WHEN THEY DO THIS.

Now arrange the circled letters to form the surprise answer, as suggested by the above cartoon.

Print answer here “ ”

JUMBLE®

Unscramble these four Jumbles, one letter to each square, to form four ordinary words.

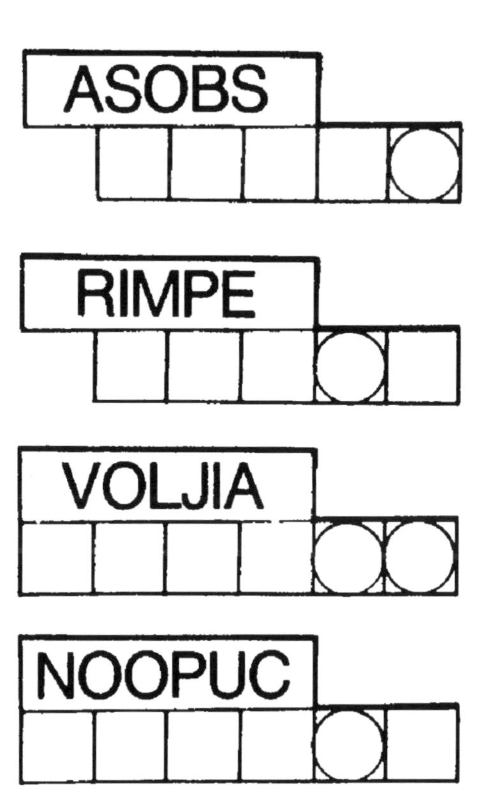
ASOBS
RIMPE
VOLJIA
NOOPUC

WHAT THE CATTLE TYCOON MADE A LOT OF.

Now arrange the circled letters to form the surprise answer, as suggested by the above cartoon.

Print answer here

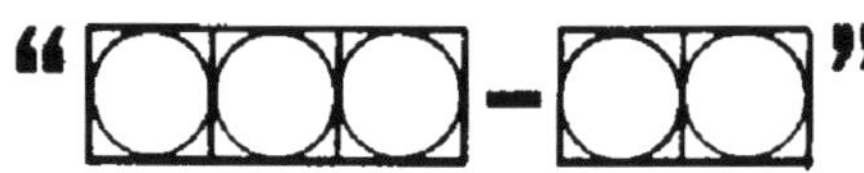

JUMBLE®

Unscramble these four Jumbles, one letter to each square, to form four ordinary words.

ANGLD
HASAW
BRENAT
GURTIA
HOW THE WINNER WAS CHOSEN AT THAT BIG ART CONTEST.
Print answer here BY

Now arrange the circled letters to form the surprise answer, as suggested by the above cartoon.

JUMBLE®

Unscramble these four Jumbles, one letter to each square, to form four ordinary words.

HAMOC
NYKAL
THACED
MUTTUL
How about a higher one?
WHAT A CLIMB UP THAT LITTLE HILL DIDN'T DO.
Print answer here
" - " TO

Now arrange the circled letters to form the surprise answer, as suggested by the above cartoon.

JUMBLE®

Unscramble these four Jumbles, one letter to each square, to form four ordinary words.

DOBOR
WICTE
CLAGEN
SMALID
WHAT THE SALES-LADY SAID WHEN ASKED WHETHER THAT NEW TYPE FOUNDATION GARMENT IS REALLY GOING TO WORK.

Now arrange the circled letters to form the surprise answer, as suggested by the above cartoon.

Print answer here "OF ▢▢▢▢-▢▢" ▢▢▢▢▢

JUMBLE®

Unscramble these four Jumbles, one letter to each square, to form four ordinary words.

MACHP
PUJMY
RESTUM
BRUNKE
WHAT SHE DOES WHEN SHE KISSES HER HOCKEY PLAYER BOYFRIEND.

Now arrange the circled letters to form the surprise answer, as suggested by the above cartoon.

Print answer here “ - ”

JUMBLE®

Unscramble these four Jumbles, one letter to each square, to form four ordinary words.

LIWLT
CYDUH
SAMOUF
RAAPPE
WHAT HAPPENED WHEN THE SAFETY MATCH TYCOON LOST HIS TEMPER?

Now arrange the circled letters to form the surprise answer, as suggested by the above cartoon.

Print answer here HE

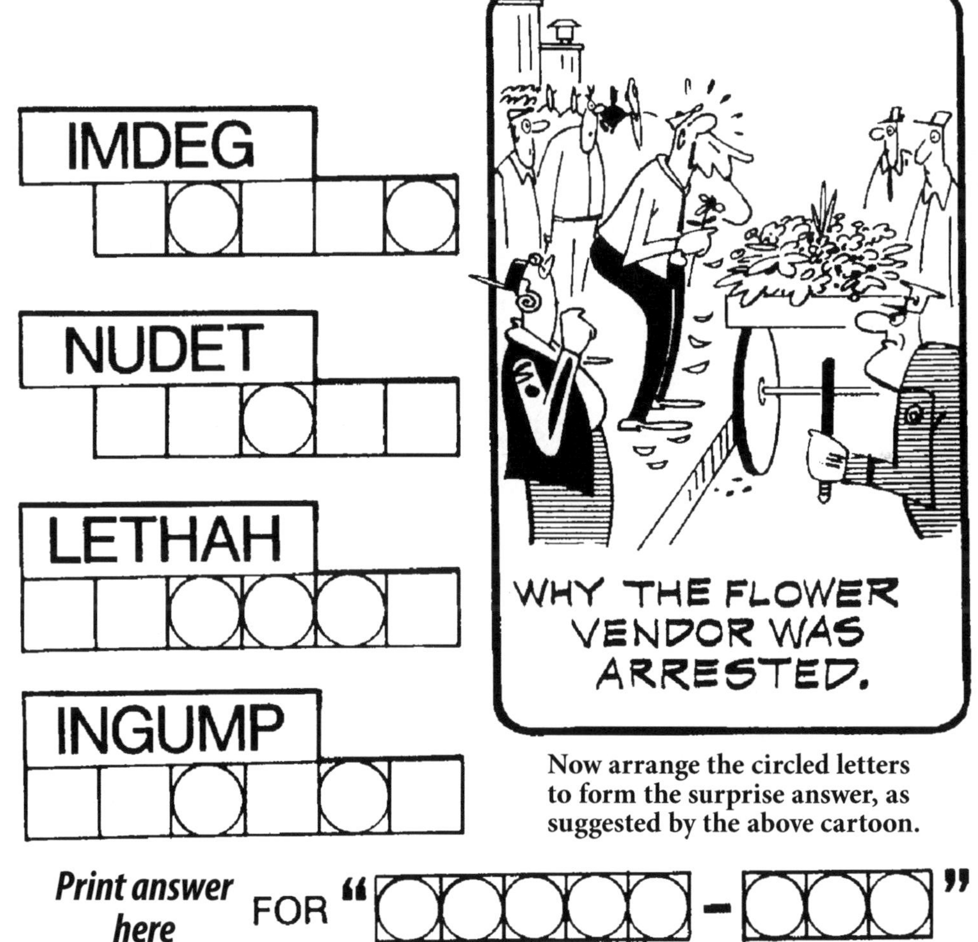
JUMBLE®
Unscramble these four Jumbles, one letter to each square, to form four ordinary words.
IMDEG
NUDET
LETHAH
INGUMP
WHY THE FLOWER VENDOR WAS ARRESTED.
Now arrange the circled letters to form the surprise answer, as suggested by the above cartoon.
Print answer here
FOR " - "

JUMBLE®

Unscramble these four Jumbles, one letter to each square, to form four ordinary words.

GITHE
TRONS
THUBOG
OCTIXE
WHEN HIS TONGUE IS LOOSE, IT'S OFTEN BECAUSE HE IS THIS.

Now arrange the circled letters to form the surprise answer, as suggested by the above cartoon.

Print answer here “ ◯◯◯◯◯ ”

JUMBLE®

Unscramble these four Jumbles, one letter to each square, to form four ordinary words.

LENEK
NAHDY
SYMFLE
TARIPE
I feel funny
MURDER
ROBBERY
WHAT THOSE CORDUROY PILLOWS MADE.

Now arrange the circled letters to form the surprise answer, as suggested by the above cartoon.

Print answer here

JUMBLE®

Unscramble these four Jumbles, one letter to each square, to form four ordinary words.

HOPOW

RABOX

JINTEC

MERMAH

Yes, sir . . .
No, sir . . .
Sorry, sir . . .
Won't happen again, sir . . .
The old man is chewing him out
WHAT KIND OF A PROBLEM DID THE CAPTAIN FACE?

Now arrange the circled letters to form the surprise answer, as suggested by the above cartoon.

Print answer here A " "

PUZZLE
63

JUMBLE®

Unscramble these four Jumbles, one letter to each square, to form four ordinary words.

FUINY

BOESE

YATGIE

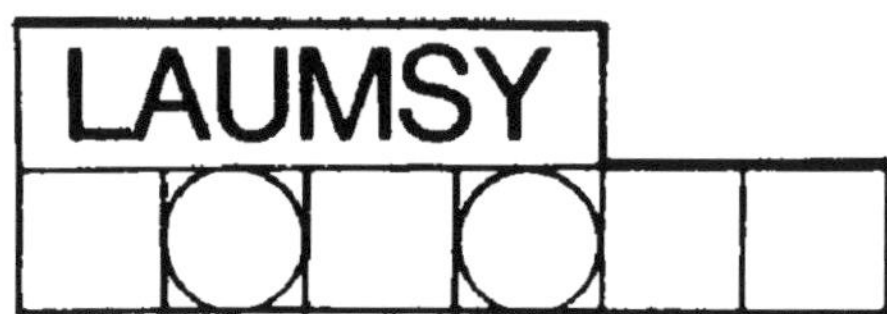
LAUMSY

WHY THE CARPENTER NEEDED ALL THAT EMERGENCY DENTAL WORK.

Now arrange the circled letters to form the surprise answer, as suggested by the above cartoon.

Print answer here HE  HIS 

JUMBLE®

Unscramble these four Jumbles, one letter to each square, to form four ordinary words.

INVEA
TUDOO
FARGOE
DIAMER
Nobody's called me today
WHAT YOUR TELEPHONE MIGHT BECOME IF YOU FAIL TO PAY THE BILL.

Now arrange the circled letters to form the surprise answer, as suggested by the above cartoon.

Print answer here A

JUMBLE®

Unscramble these four Jumbles, one letter to each square, to form four ordinary words.

DOYNS
HOBAR
KOFERD
KALTEC
But I just wanted to go out for some air
WHY THE EMPLOYEE AT THE CAR FACTORY WAS FIRED.
Now arrange the circled letters to form the surprise answer, as suggested by the above cartoon.
Print answer here
HE
A “ ”

JUMBLE®

Unscramble these four Jumbles, one letter to each square, to form four ordinary words.

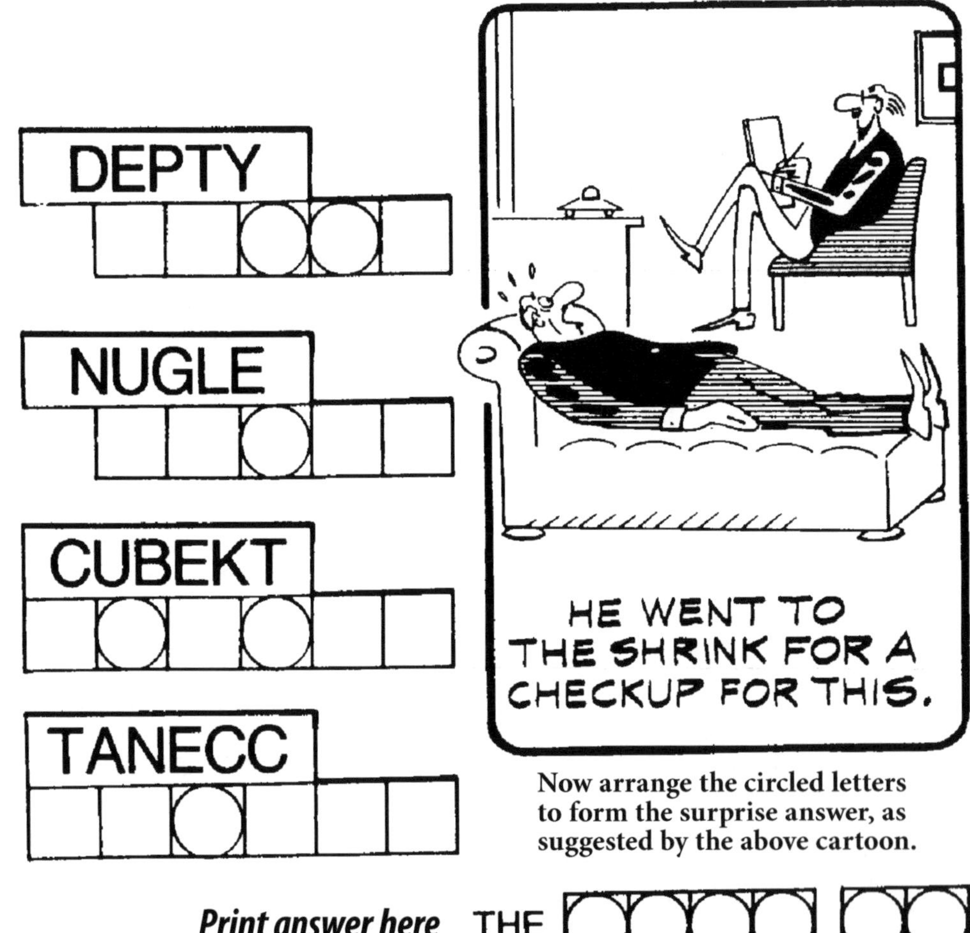
DEPTY
NUGLE
CUBEKT
TANECC
HE WENT TO
THE SHRINK FOR A
CHECKUP FOR THIS.

Now arrange the circled letters to form the surprise answer, as suggested by the above cartoon.

Print answer here THE

JUMBLE®

Unscramble these four Jumbles, one letter to each square, to form four ordinary words.

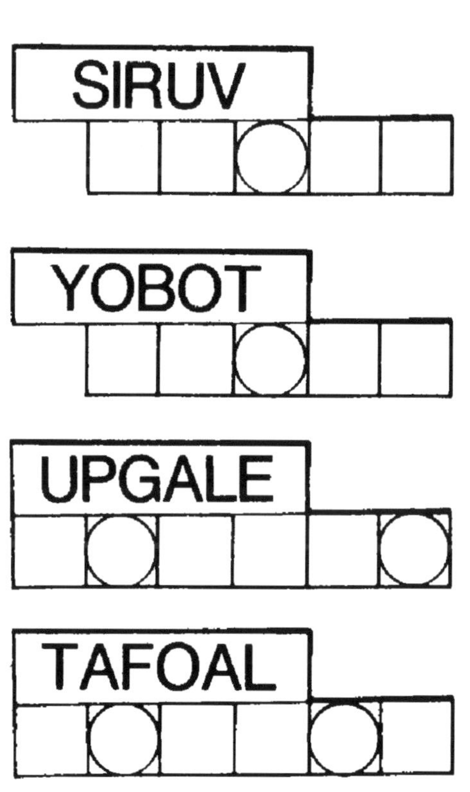
SIRUV
YOBOT
UPGALE
TAFOAL

THE BAKER HIRED — AND THEN FIRED —

Now arrange the circled letters to form the surprise answer, as suggested by the above cartoon.

Print answer here A "◯◯◯◯-◯◯"

JUMBLE®

Unscramble these four Jumbles, one letter to each square, to form four ordinary words.

ENGAM
WESHO
TICUND
DOUXES
FOR NOT SHOVELING THE SIDEWALK THERE —
Now arrange the circled letters to form the surprise answer, as suggested by the above cartoon.
Print answer here

JUMBLE®

Unscramble these four Jumbles, one letter to each square, to form four ordinary words.

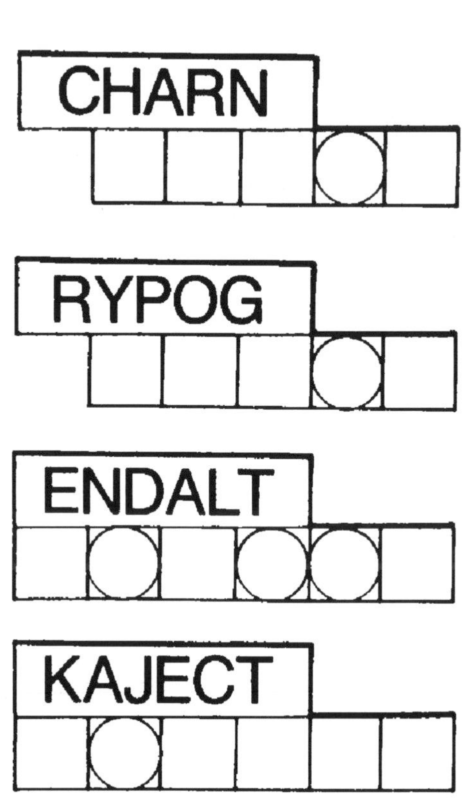
CHARN
RYPOG
ENDALT
KAJECT

WHAT SOME NOT-SO-YOUNG ACTORS FIND IT DIFFICULT TO DO.

Now arrange the circled letters to form the surprise answer, as suggested by the above cartoon.

Print answer here  THEIR 

JUMBLE®

Unscramble these four Jumbles, one letter to each square, to form four ordinary words.

TALPI
NECHE
TIFONY
INMALY
WHAT THEY CALLED THE GUY WHO WAS NUTS ABOUT FISHING.

Now arrange the circled letters to form the surprise answer, as suggested by the above cartoon.

Print answer here A “ - ”

JUMBLE®

Unscramble these four Jumbles, one letter to each square, to form four ordinary words.

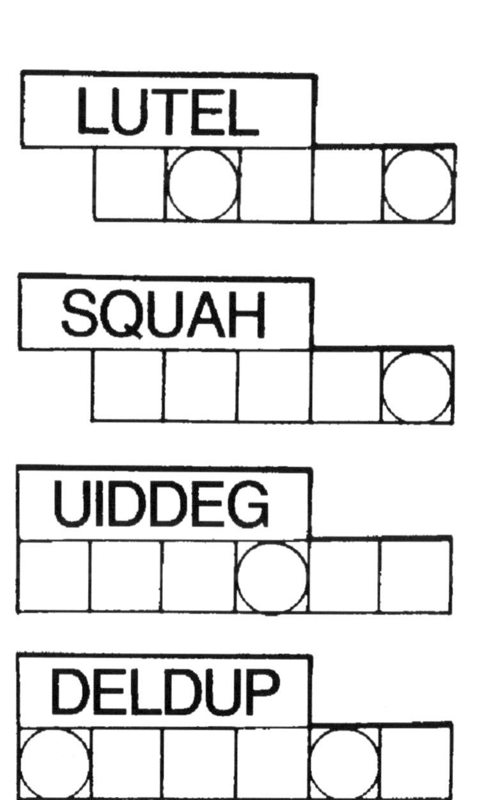
LUTEL
SQUAH
UIDDEG
DELDUP

WHAT HAPPENED AFTER HE BOUGHT A NEW PAIR OF SUSPENDERS?

Now arrange the circled letters to form the surprise answer, as suggested by the above cartoon.

Print answer here HE WAS

JUMBLE®

Unscramble these four Jumbles, one letter to each square, to form four ordinary words.

ATTIR
DOPEK
RIMMOE
CORCUN
Snap course
Even an idiot could have passed
WHAT THAT DROP-OUT FROM THE DATA PROCESSING SCHOOL MUST HAVE BEEN.
Print answer here A " - "

Now arrange the circled letters to form the surprise answer, as suggested by the above cartoon.

JUMBLE®

Unscramble these four Jumbles, one letter to each square, to form four ordinary words.

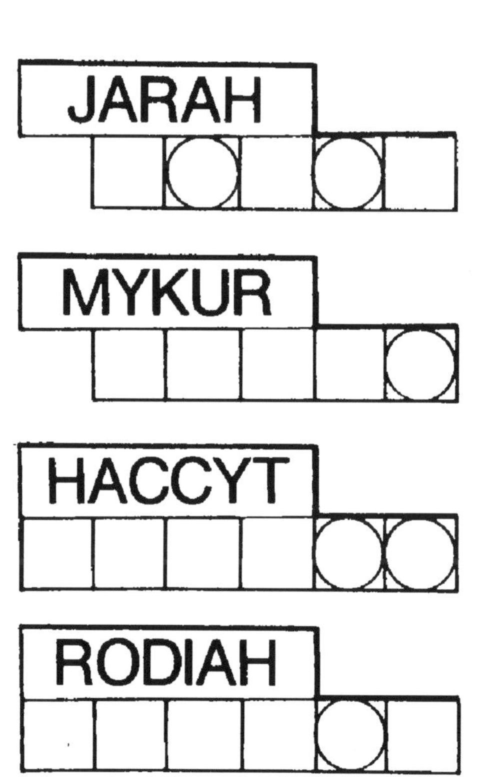
JARAH
MYKUR
HACCYT
RODIAH

IN THOSE YEARS STRAW HATS HAD THIS.

Now arrange the circled letters to form the surprise answer, as suggested by the above cartoon.

Print answer here THEIR "◯◯◯" ◯◯◯

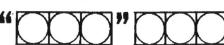

JUMBLE®

Unscramble these four Jumbles, one letter to each square, to form four ordinary words.

KOLEY
GWAON
FABFEL
IMLYRG
WHAT THAT GOLF NUT HAD IN HIS EYES.

Now arrange the circled letters to form the surprise answer, as suggested by the above cartoon.

Print answer here A "▢▢▢▢-▢▢▢" ▢▢▢▢

JUMBLE®

Unscramble these four Jumbles, one letter to each square, to form four ordinary words.

ROGOF
GIESE
LAWASY
KONVIE
WHEN THEY FILM A WINTRY SCENE IN HOLLY-WOOD, THE PROP MAN HAS TO COME UP WITH PLENTY OF THESE.

Now arrange the circled letters to form the surprise answer, as suggested by the above cartoon.

Print answer here

JUMBLE®

Unscramble these four Jumbles, one letter to each square, to form four ordinary words.

I'VE FINALLY BOUGHT YOU A WATCH FOR YOUR BIRTHDAY, DEAR
TONJI
AVVLE
STUMKE
ABHORR

Now arrange the circled letters to form the surprise answer, as suggested by the above cartoon.

Print answer here “IT'S ◯◯◯◯◯ ◯◯◯◯”

JUMBLE®

Unscramble these four Jumbles, one letter to each square, to form four ordinary words.

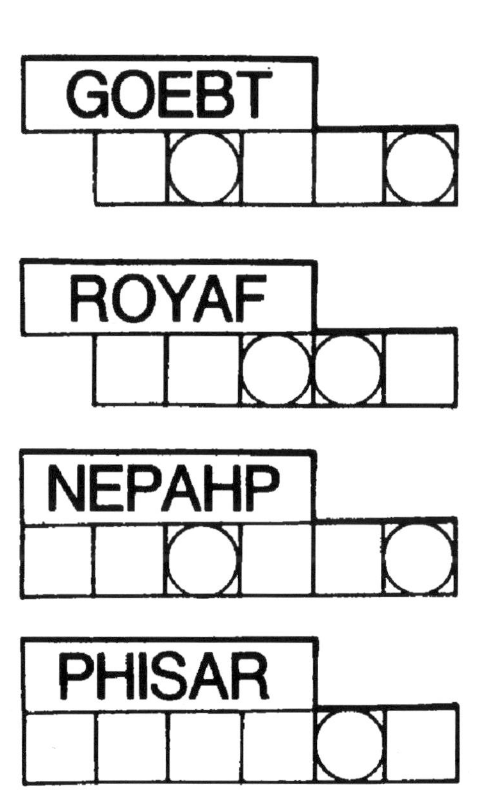
GOEBT
ROYAF
NEPAHP
PHISAR

FOOTWEA
THE ONLY THING THAT CHILDREN WEAR OUT FASTER THAN SHOES.

Now arrange the circled letters to form the surprise answer, as suggested by the above cartoon.

Print answer here

JUMBLE®

Unscramble these four Jumbles, one letter to each square, to form four ordinary words.

GANET

SOUHE

LYNFOD

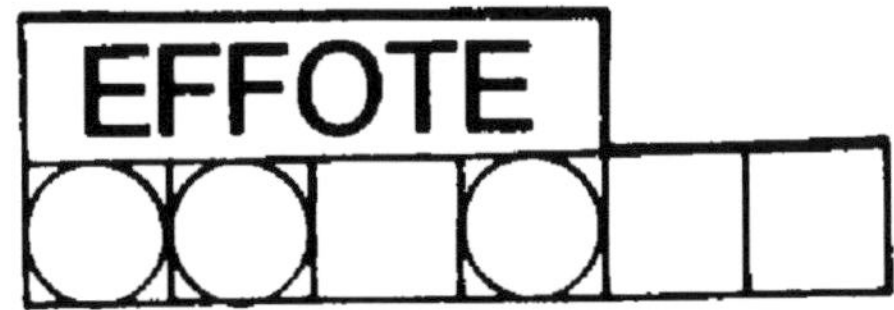
EFFOTE

WELL!
HOW THE TRAFFIC COP'S GIRLFRIEND CAUGHT HIM.

Now arrange the circled letters to form the surprise answer, as suggested by the above cartoon.

Print answer here

JUMBLE®

Unscramble these four Jumbles, one letter to each square, to form four ordinary words.

JEDDA
GNATY
COBORN
NAVIED
THE MEDIA THOUGHT THEY'D BETTER GIVE THE EVENT PLENTY OF THIS.

Now arrange the circled letters to form the surprise answer, as suggested by the above cartoon.

Print answer here " ○○○○○○○○ "

JUMBLE®

Unscramble these four Jumbles, one letter to each square, to form four ordinary words.

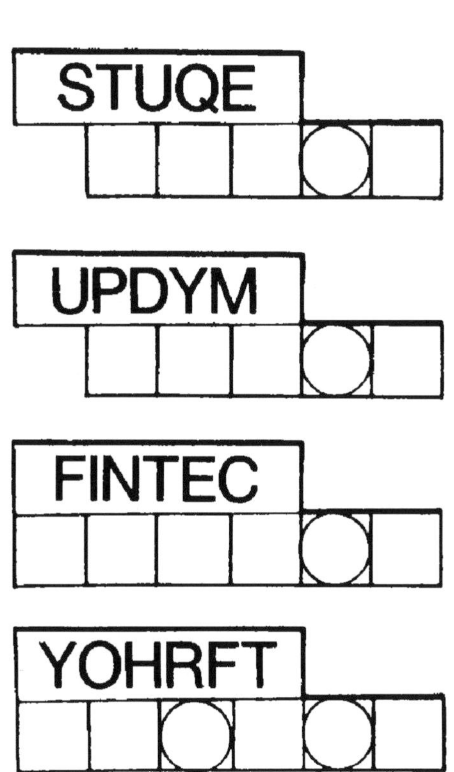
STUQE
UPDYM
FINTEC
YOHRFT

WHAT THE KARATE CHAMP TURNED RESTAURANT OWNER SPECIALIZED IN.

Now arrange the circled letters to form the surprise answer, as suggested by the above cartoon.

Print answer here 

JUMBLE®

Unscramble these four Jumbles, one letter to each square, to form four ordinary words.

PERIT
HISFY
SNIULF
NITIVE
HAPPY NEW YEAR!
HOW THEY CELE-BRATED THE NEW YEAR AT THAT OLD-TIME SALOON.

Now arrange the circled letters to form the surprise answer, as suggested by the above cartoon.

Print answer here WITH " - "

JUMBLE®

Unscramble these four Jumbles, one letter to each square, to form four ordinary words.

PRUTE

NUGOY

NERUNG

RAYTLE

A MAN SOLD ME THE NILE RIVER FOR TEN DOLLARS

Now arrange the circled letters to form the surprise answer, as suggested by the above cartoon.

Print answer here "◯-◯◯◯◯" ◯◯◯

JUMBLE®

Unscramble these four Jumbles, one letter to each square, to form four ordinary words.

TIFFY
IRROG
DRAIMY
LIDIAN
I wish others would also be concerned about the neighborhood
SOMEBODY WHO CALLS A SPADE A SPADE MIGHT WANT TO GIVE YOU THIS.

Now arrange the circled letters to form the surprise answer, as suggested by the above cartoon.

Print answer here A ◯◯◯◯◯ "◯◯◯"

PUZZLE
84

JUMBLE®

Unscramble these four Jumbles, one letter to each square, to form four ordinary words.

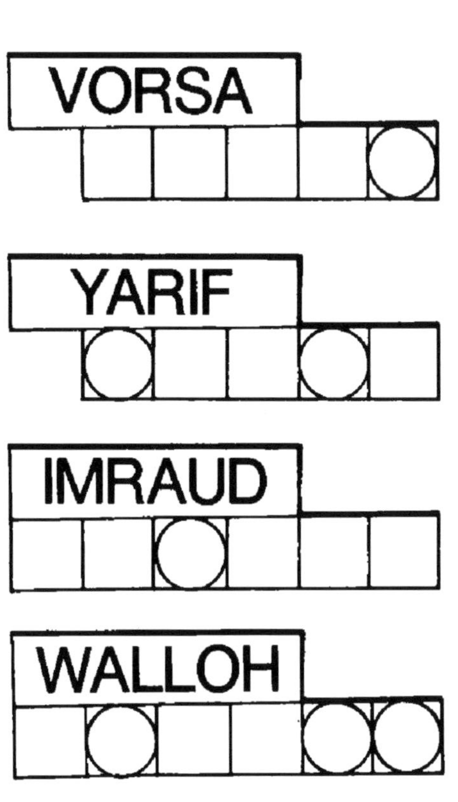
VORSA
YARIF
IMRAUD
WALLOH

Hey—how about a raise?
A LIVE WIRE IS NEVER BACKWARD IN GOING THERE.

Now arrange the circled letters to form the surprise answer, as suggested by the above cartoon.

Print answer here 

JUMBLE®

Unscramble these four Jumbles, one letter to each square, to form four ordinary words.

EUQUE

REBET

PHORGE

MEESID

He's as powerful as any ruler in history
WHAT THE ROPE TYCOON BUILT.

Now arrange the circled letters to form the surprise answer, as suggested by the above cartoon.

Print answer here A HUGE "[ ][ ][ ][ ]-[ ][ ][ ]"

JUMBLE®

Unscramble these four Jumbles, one letter to each square, to form four ordinary words.

MARDA

PITED

CRUSIC

INVOCE

I don't understand this
WHAT YOU SHOULD GET BEFORE IN-VESTING IN EXPENSIVE AUDIO EQUIPMENT.

Now arrange the circled letters to form the surprise answer, as suggested by the above cartoon.

Print answer here " "

JUMBLE®

Unscramble these four Jumbles, one letter to each square, to form four ordinary words.

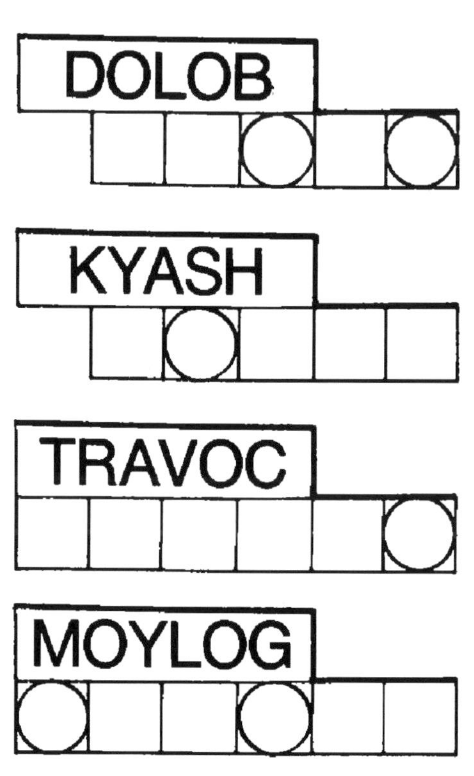
DOLOB
KYASH
TRAVOC
MOYLOG

HE WON THE BIGGEST BET AT THE GREYHOUND RACE BECAUSE HE HAD THIS.

Now arrange the circled letters to form the surprise answer, as suggested by the above cartoon.

Print answer here A

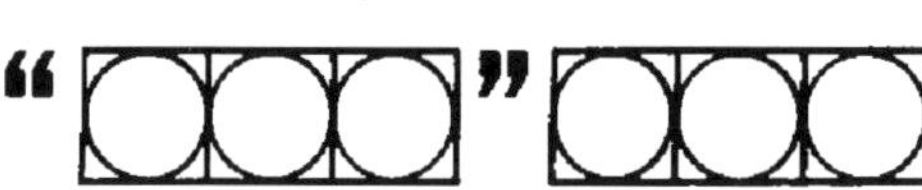

JUMBLE®

Unscramble these four Jumbles, one letter to each square, to form four ordinary words.

AUZER
PAWMS
FUALED
YAPNOC
He'd do a lot of good if he weren't so long-winded
WHAT MANY A PUBLIC SPEAKER DEVOTES HIS LIFE TO.
Now arrange the circled letters to form the surprise answer, as suggested by the above cartoon.
Print answer here
A " "

JUMBLE®

Unscramble these four Jumbles, one letter to each square, to form four ordinary words.

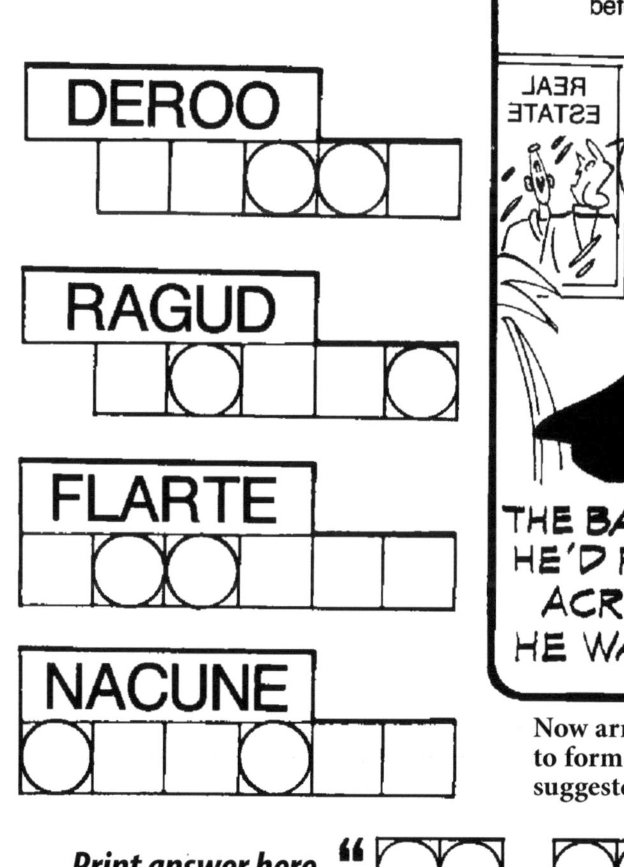
DEROO
RAGUD
FLARTE
NACUNE

Might as well take the plunge before I acquire any other responsibilities
REAL ESTATE
He's worth catching
THE BACHELOR THOUGHT HE'D PURCHASE SOME ACREAGE WHILE HE WAS STILL THIS.

Now arrange the circled letters to form the surprise answer, as suggested by the above cartoon.

Print answer here " ◯◯-◯◯◯◯◯◯ "

JUMBLE®

Unscramble these four Jumbles, one letter to each square, to form four ordinary words.

NIFET

YANNO

DINGHI

TEXMEP

One degree above zero
So what? Who cares?
WHAT BITTER COLD WEATHER SOMETIMES IS.

Now arrange the circled letters to form the surprise answer, as suggested by the above cartoon.

Print answer here TO " "

JUMBLE®

Unscramble these four Jumbles, one letter to each square, to form four ordinary words.

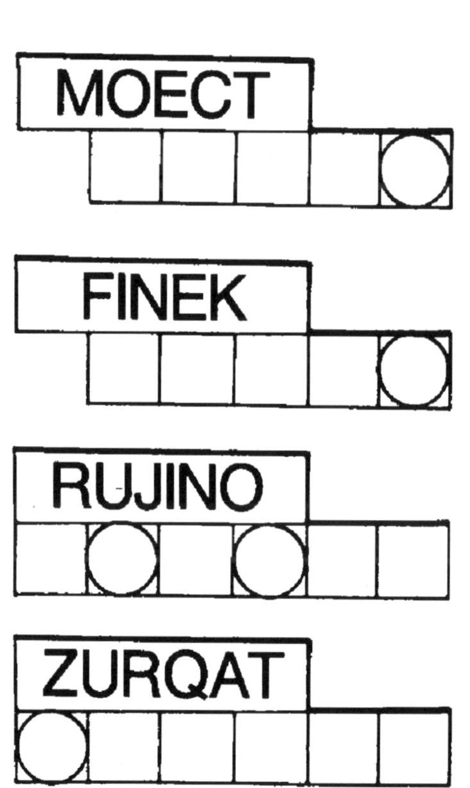
MOECT
FINEK
RUJINO
ZURQAT

YAK YAK YAK
A GUY SHOULD BE THIS WHEN HE GOES ON A DIET.

Now arrange the circled letters to form the surprise answer, as suggested by the above cartoon.

Print answer here 

JUMBLE®

Unscramble these four Jumbles, one letter to each square, to form four ordinary words.

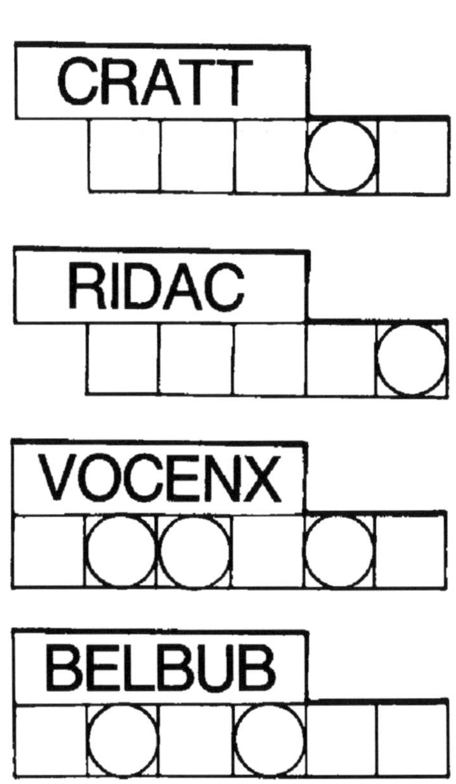
CRATT
RIDAC
VOCENX
BELBUB

Got to get rid of this ham
WHAT THE INDIA RUBBER MAN AT THE CIRCUS GOT.

Now arrange the circled letters to form the surprise answer, as suggested by the above cartoon.

Print answer here

JUMBLE®

Unscramble these four Jumbles, one letter to each square, to form four ordinary words.

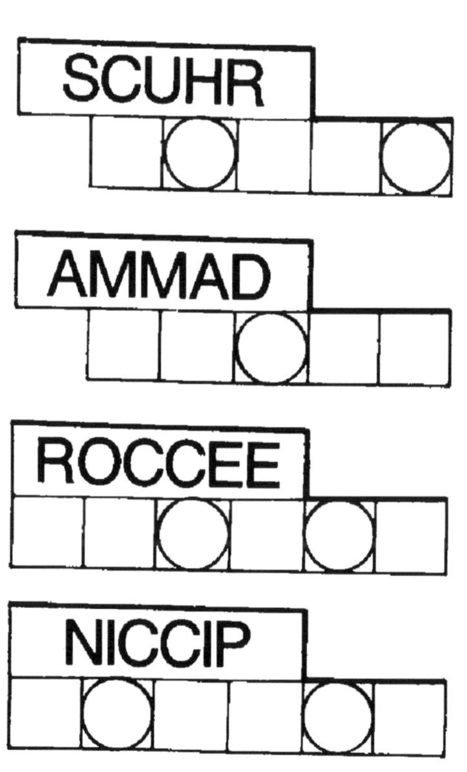
SCUHR
AMMAD
ROCCEE
NICCIP

I'm getting hungry
Here's a quarter, go get me the special sandwich at that greasy spoon
A MISER LIVES POOR SO HE CAN DO THIS.

Now arrange the circled letters to form the surprise answer, as suggested by the above cartoon.

Print answer here

JUMBLE®

Unscramble these four Jumbles, one letter to each square, to form four ordinary words.

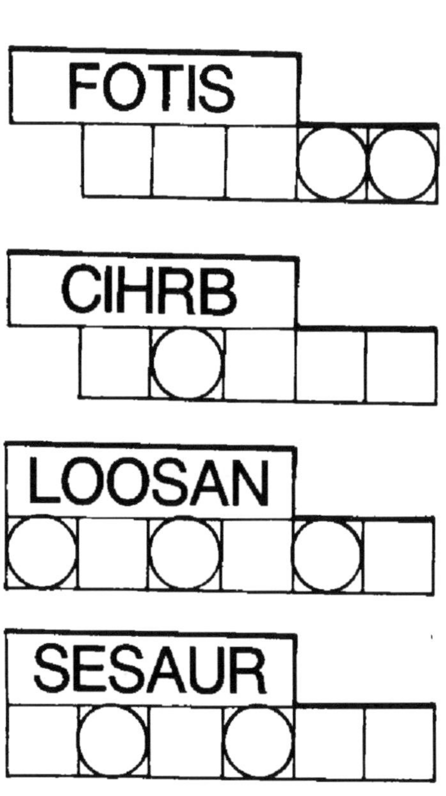
FOTIS
CIHRB
LOOSAN
SESAUR

We won—but after the legal expenses, I don't know...
THESE WORDS SOMETIMES DESCRIBE A LAW SUIT.

Now arrange the circled letters to form the surprise answer, as suggested by the above cartoon.

Print answer here A

JUMBLE®

Unscramble these four Jumbles, one letter to each square, to form four ordinary words.

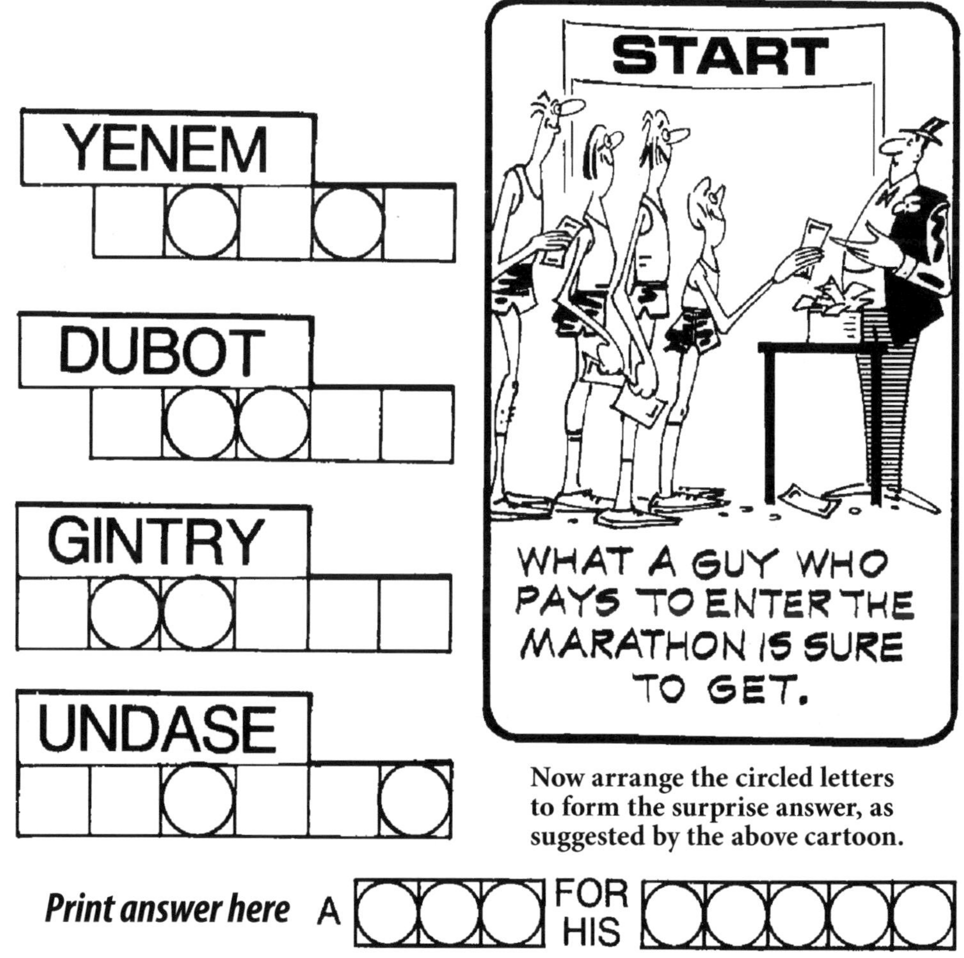
YENEM
DUBOT
GINTRY
UNDASE
START
WHAT A GUY WHO PAYS TO ENTER THE MARATHON IS SURE TO GET.

Now arrange the circled letters to form the surprise answer, as suggested by the above cartoon.

Print answer here A ◯◯◯ FOR HIS ◯◯◯◯◯

JUMBLE®

Unscramble these four Jumbles, one letter to each square, to form four ordinary words.

ANUFA
VAYEH
REMMOY
TAUMUN
Disgraceful
POLLUTION IS THE CONTAMINATION OF NATURE BY THIS.

Now arrange the circled letters to form the surprise answer, as suggested by the above cartoon.

Print answer here

JUMBLE®

Unscramble these four Jumbles, one letter to each square, to form four ordinary words.

YONOL
INBAR
GUDEMS
STOLCY
WHERE YOU MIGHT FIND THOSE OPTOMETRY STUDENTS.

Now arrange the circled letters to form the surprise answer, as suggested by the above cartoon.

Print answer here IN THE " "

JUMBLE®

Unscramble these four Jumbles, one letter to each square, to form four ordinary words.

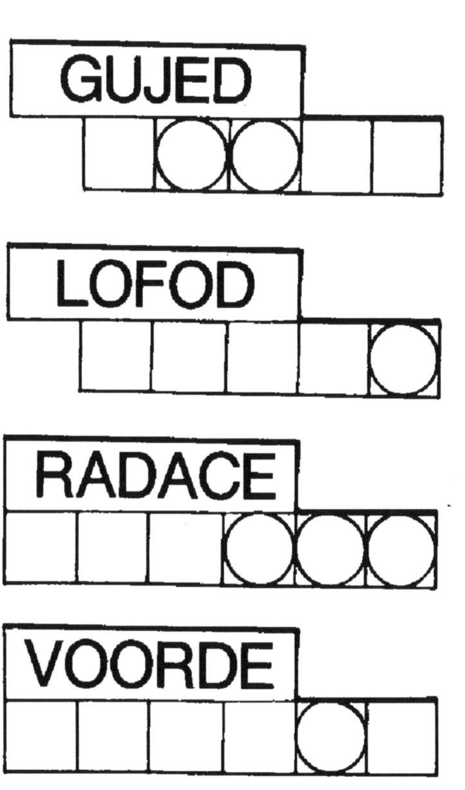
GUJED
LOFOD
RADACE
VOORDE

That's my pop!
APPROPRIATE FOR THE GUY WHO WINS THE COWBOY-FATHER-OF-THE-YEAR AWARD.

Now arrange the circled letters to form the surprise answer, as suggested by the above cartoon.

Print answer here A "◯◯◯◯-◯◯◯"

JUMBLE®

Unscramble these four Jumbles, one letter to each square, to form four ordinary words.

FEACH

NORDE

DISMOW

TIRRAY

Sunny all day
HE'S SOMETIMES WEATHER-WISE, BUT MORE OFTEN THIS.

Now arrange the circled letters to form the surprise answer, as suggested by the above cartoon.

Print answer here

JUMBLE®

Unscramble these four Jumbles, one letter to each square, to form four ordinary words.

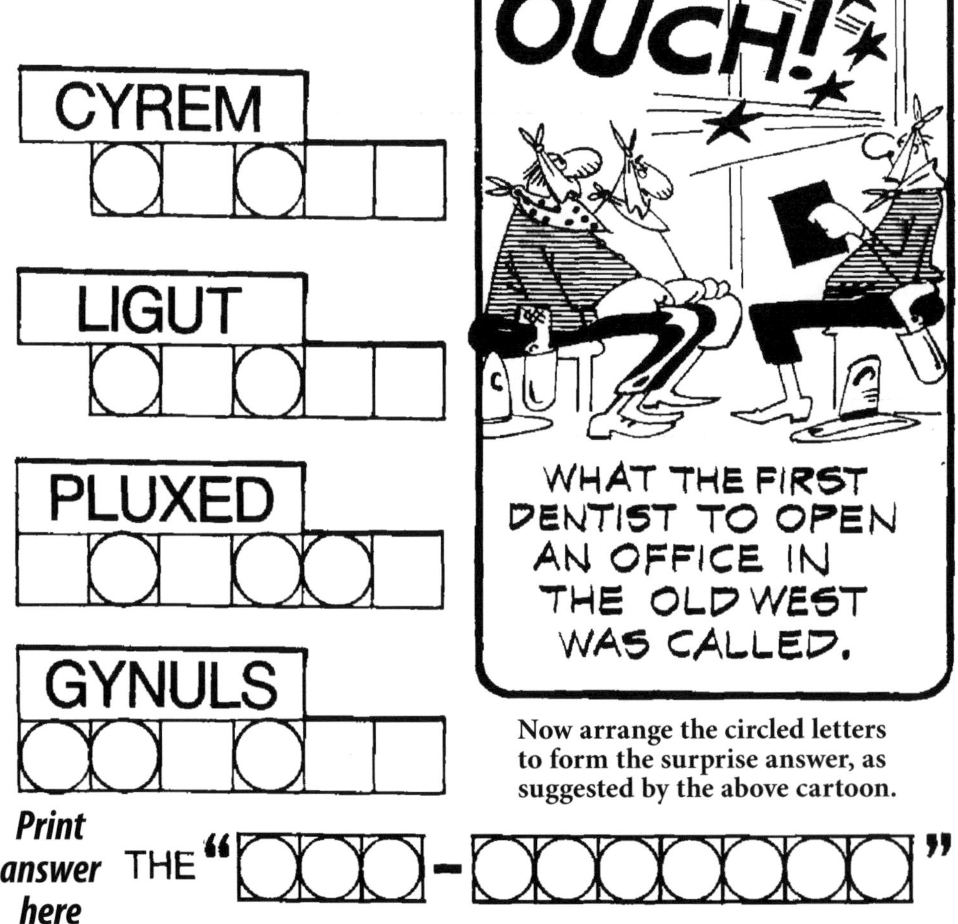
CYREM
LIGUT
PLUXED
GYNULS
OUCH!
WHAT THE FIRST DENTIST TO OPEN AN OFFICE IN THE OLD WEST WAS CALLED.

Now arrange the circled letters to form the surprise answer, as suggested by the above cartoon.

Print answer here THE "☐☐☐-☐☐☐☐☐☐☐"

JUMBLE®

Unscramble these four Jumbles, one letter to each square, to form four ordinary words.

BROTI
UYOSP
TUSHIA
YGANIS
How's your wine?
I think I'll only need one glass tonight.
I can barely lift this.
I love this place!
THEY LOVED THE NEW WINE BAR AND ITS ---

Now arrange the circled letters to form the surprise answer, as suggested by the above cartoon.

Print answer here ○○○ "○○○○○-○○○○○○"

JUMBLE®

Unscramble these four Jumbles, one letter to each square, to form four ordinary words.

TAYRP

NFGIL

VOITEM

HRALEB

Kids, did you know that Big Ben's accurate to within one second?
I can't even think of another clock I've wanted to see so much.
BIG BEN MAY BE THE MOST FAMOUS CLOCK ---

Now arrange the circled letters to form the surprise answer, as suggested by the above cartoon.

Print answer here

JUMBLE®

Unscramble these four Jumbles, one letter to each square, to form four ordinary words.

GANCO

SNAPT

ORETES

CICHET

I have a package for 2-B. Can you sign for it?
No. Tenants need to sign for their own packages.
Huge Prime
No Solicitati
THE LANDLORD WOULDN'T SIGN FOR TENANTS' PACKAGES, ---

Now arrange the circled letters to form the surprise answer, as suggested by the above cartoon.

Print answer here “ ”

JUMBLE®
Unscramble these four Jumbles, one letter to each square, to form four ordinary words.
IRECI
KORJE
GAMEAD
CODENS
Let's concentrate on your favorite subjects.
It's hard to choose between art and science.
Well, you could study industrial design like me, or nursing like your mother.
SWIM
DECIDING WHAT TO STUDY IN COLLEGE CAN BE A --
Print answer here

Now arrange the circled letters to form the surprise answer, as suggested by the above cartoon.

JUMBLE®

Unscramble these four Jumbles, one letter to each square, to form four ordinary words.

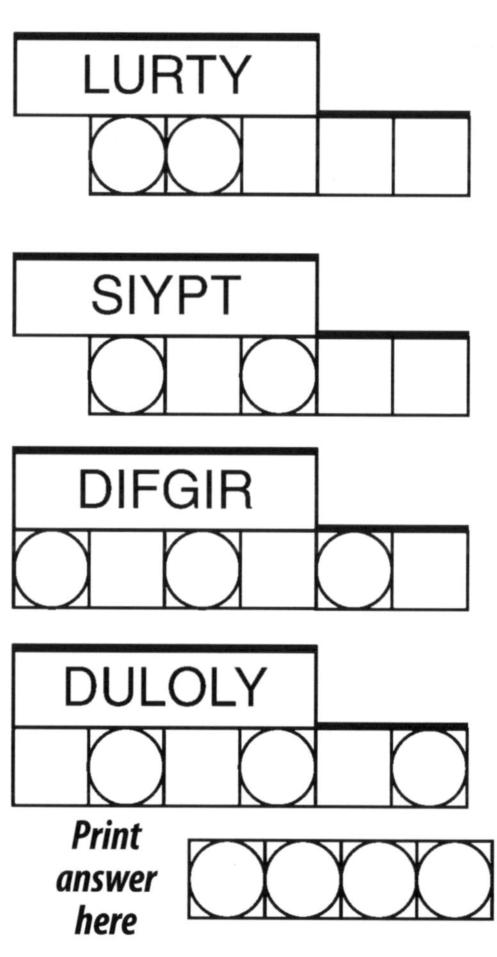
LURTY
SIYPT
DIFGIR
DULOLY

Here's your money. You must really clean up.
My business does pretty well.
THE OWNER OF THE MAID SERVICE WAS MAKING A ----

Now arrange the circled letters to form the surprise answer, as suggested by the above cartoon.

Print answer here

JUMBLE®

Unscramble these four Jumbles, one letter to each square, to form four ordinary words.

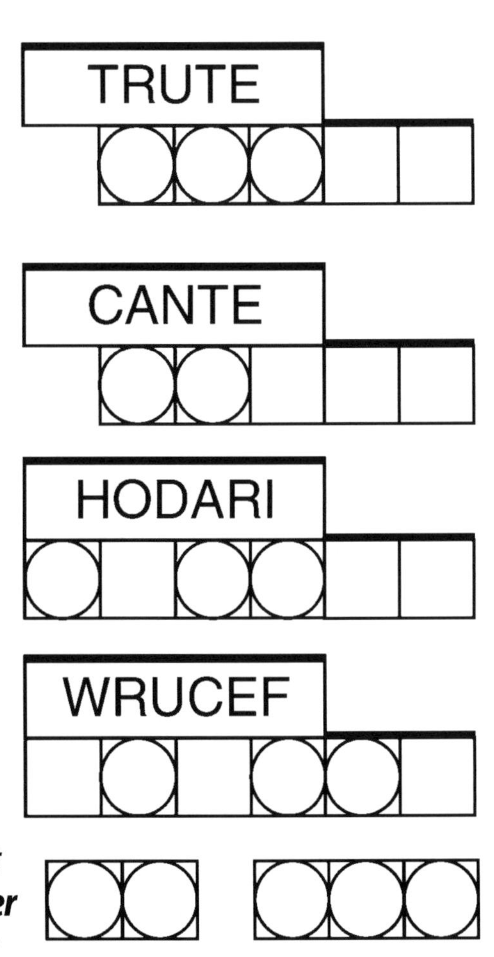
TRUTE
CANTE
HODARI
WRUCEF

Oh, no! It says here that they're canceling the show!
Maybe they can make movies one day.
Where am I going to wear my costume?
"STAR TREK" WAS CANCELED AFTER THREE SEASONS, BUT ITS SUCCESS WAS SET ---

Now arrange the circled letters to form the surprise answer, as suggested by the above cartoon.

Print answer here

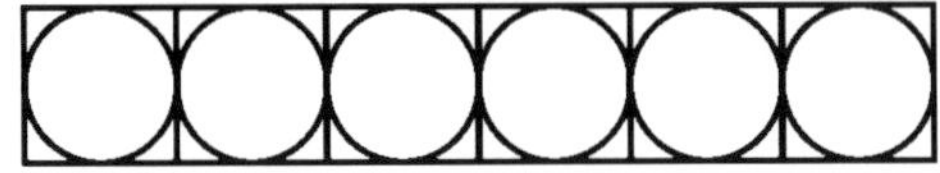

JUMBLE®

Unscramble these four Jumbles, one letter to each square, to form four ordinary words.

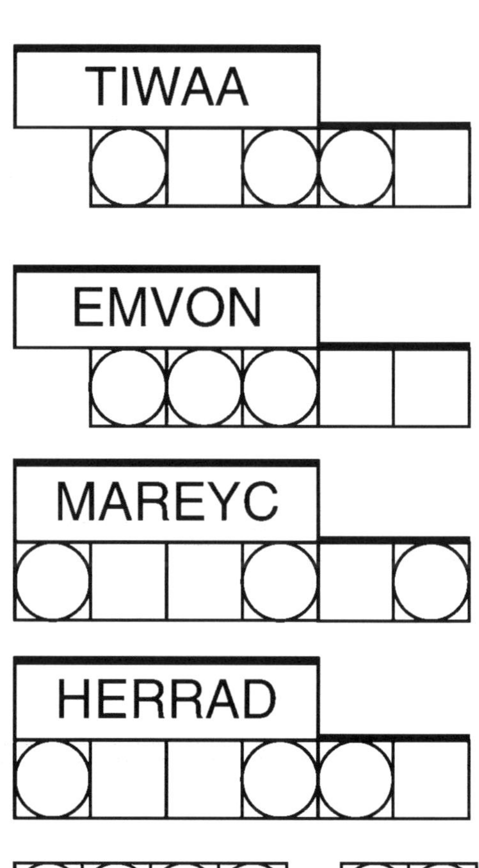
TIWAA
EMVON
MAREYC
HERRAD

Are you ready to go?
I'm going to head out. I'll see you tonight.
I'll watch the eggs. You enjoy yourself.
WHEN THE PENGUIN LEFT TO HANG OUT WITH HIS BUDDIES, HIS WIFE SAID ---

Now arrange the circled letters to form the surprise answer, as suggested by the above cartoon.

Print answer here

JUMBLE®

Unscramble these four Jumbles, one letter to each square, to form four ordinary words.

EDOMM
TYDRA
SPOMIE
AAGGRE
What do you say we all go for a walk?
You know our show is on.
We never miss it.
MAYBE THE REASON SOME PEOPLE WATCH TOO MUCH TV IS THAT THEY ARE ---

Now arrange the circled letters to form the surprise answer, as suggested by the above cartoon.

Print answer here

JUMBLE®

Unscramble these four Jumbles, one letter to each square, to form four ordinary words.

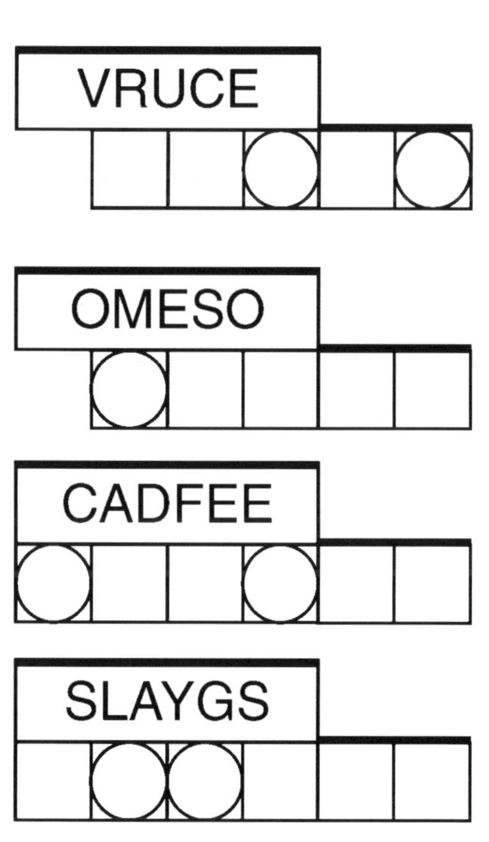
VRUCE
OMESO
CADFEE
SLAYGS

Your neighbors have installed this model.
I hope it works.
The amount of break-ins has gotten scary.
CRIME WAS ON THE RISE AND SOME PEOPLE WERE BECOMING ---

Now arrange the circled letters to form the surprise answer, as suggested by the above cartoon.

Print answer here 

JUMBLE®

Unscramble these four Jumbles, one letter to each square, to form four ordinary words.

IMERG

OTAUB

THIGST

CERNDH

I have another one.
I can't take it anymore.
This has got to stop!
WHEN THEY FOUND LISTENING DEVICES IN THEIR OFFICE, ---

Now arrange the circled letters to form the surprise answer, as suggested by the above cartoon.

Print answer here

JUMBLE®

Unscramble these four Jumbles, one letter to each square, to form four ordinary words.

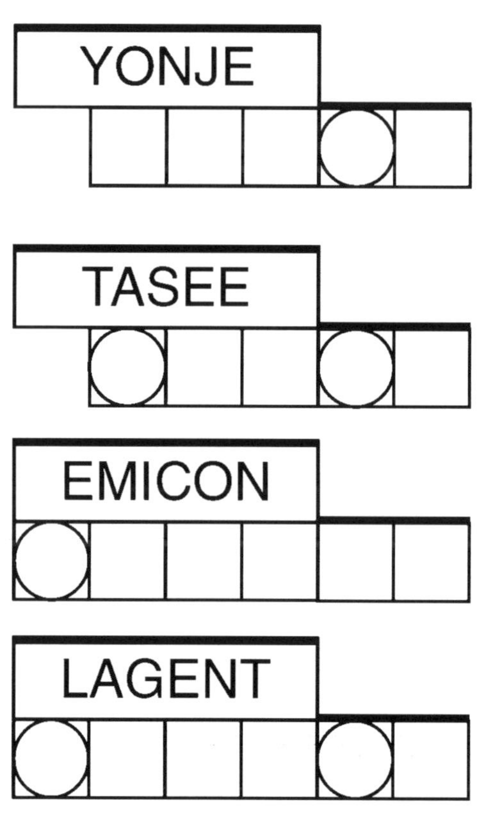
YONJE
TASEE
EMICON
LAGENT

How can you idiots not find it? Were you drunk when you made that map?

Does this say 10 paces or 70?

WHEN THE PIRATE SAW THE TREASURE WASN'T WHERE THE MAP SAID, HE ---

Now arrange the circled letters to form the surprise answer, as suggested by the above cartoon.

Print answer here  

JUMBLE®

Unscramble these four Jumbles, one letter to each square, to form four ordinary words.

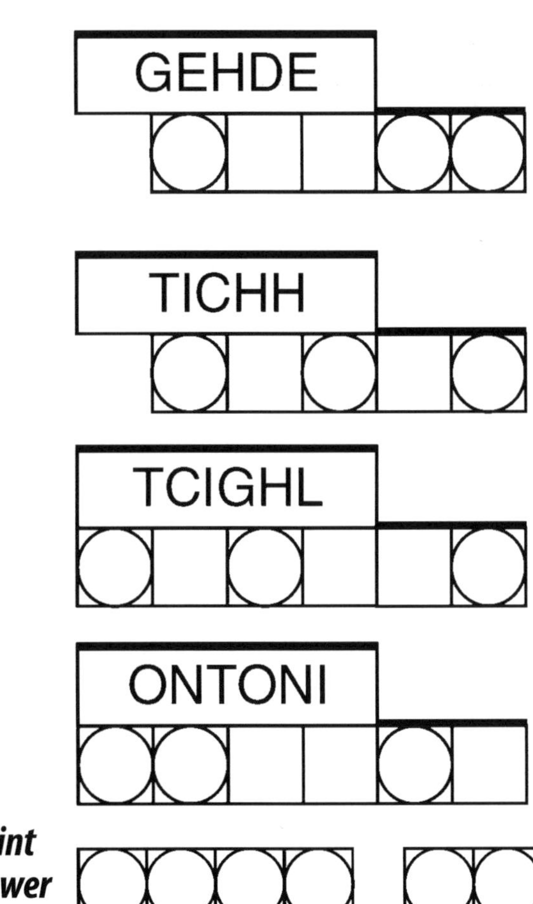
GEHDE
TICHH
TCIGHL
ONTONI

Your place is amazing! Something smells good.
Did you enjoy my limo? Champagne?
PORKY PIG'S SUCCESS MADE IT POSSIBLE FOR HIM TO LIVE ---

Now arrange the circled letters to form the surprise answer, as suggested by the above cartoon.

Print answer here

JUMBLE®

Unscramble these four Jumbles, one letter to each square, to form four ordinary words.

HIYTC
OGIGN
PWHEEN
CLORSL
His résumé is impressive.
When he's finished, bury him next to my chamber.
WHEN THE PHARAOH EMPLOYED AN ARTIST TO DECORATE HIS TOMB, IT WAS A CASE OF ---

Now arrange the circled letters to form the surprise answer, as suggested by the above cartoon.

Print answer here "◯◯◯◯-◯-◯◯◯◯◯◯◯◯"

PUZZLE
114

JUMBLE®

Unscramble these four Jumbles, one letter to each square, to form four ordinary words.

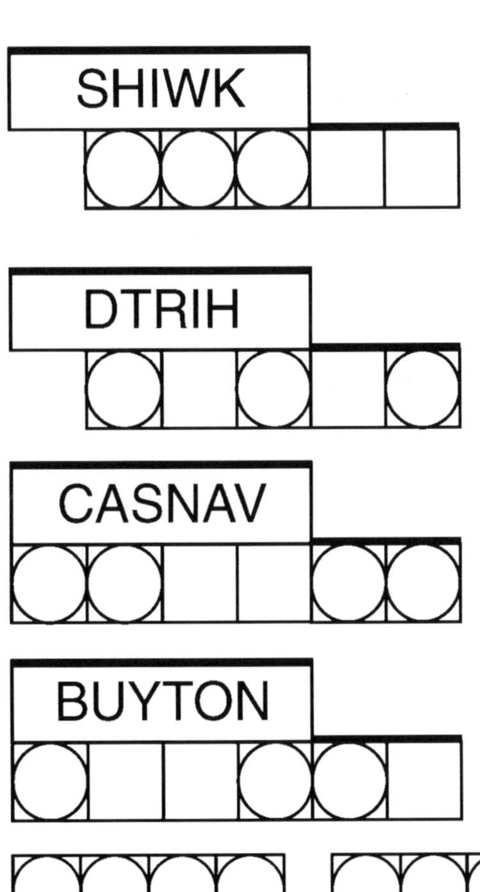
SHIWK
DTRIH
CASNAV
BUYTON

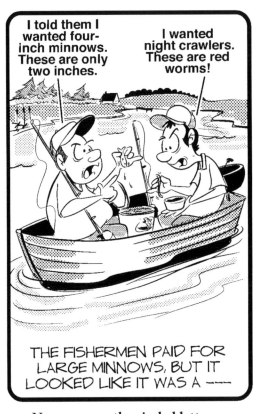

I told them I wanted four-inch minnows. These are only two inches.

I wanted night crawlers. These are red worms!

THE FISHERMEN PAID FOR LARGE MINNOWS, BUT IT LOOKED LIKE IT WAS A ---

Now arrange the circled letters to form the surprise answer, as suggested by the above cartoon.

Print answer here

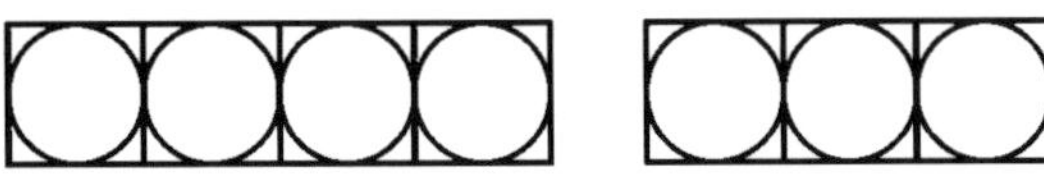

JUMBLE®

Unscramble these four Jumbles, one letter to each square, to form four ordinary words.

SMOPT
SUPAE
SPYIMK
TUQAEE
WHEN MICKEY NEEDED TO SNEAK BACK INTO THE HOUSE, HE WAS ---

Now arrange the circled letters to form the surprise answer, as suggested by the above cartoon.

Print answer here

JUMBLE®

Unscramble these four Jumbles, one letter to each square, to form four ordinary words.

NUYGO

DEWGE

TEFSAY

GRAAJU

You're in luck. Today's special is buy one lunch item, get one free.
We'll have a couple of burgers.
And milkshakes.
Jumble Diner
Jumble Diner
WHEN THE TWINS ORDERED THE "BUY ONE, GET ONE FREE" LUNCH SPECIAL, IT WAS ---

Now arrange the circled letters to form the surprise answer, as suggested by the above cartoon.

Print answer here "◯◯◯◯ - ◯◯◯"

PUZZLE 117

JUMBLE®

Unscramble these four Jumbles, one letter to each square, to form four ordinary words.

YEXOP
SUYBH
TOONIM
DEEELN

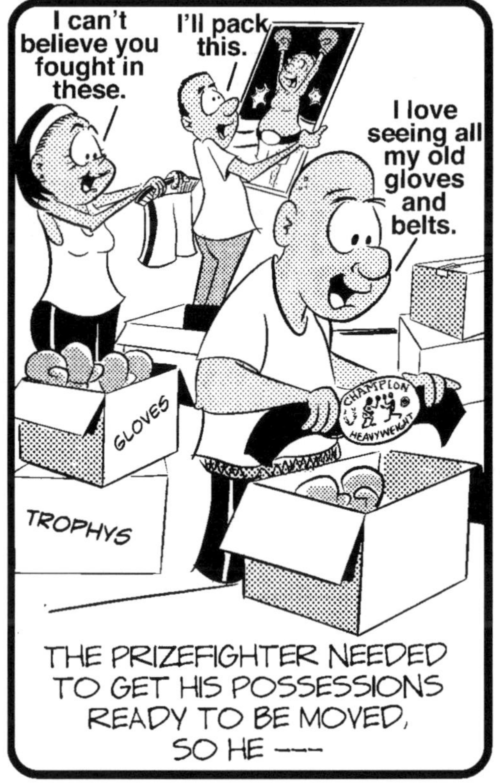

I can't believe you fought in these.
I'll pack this.
I love seeing all my old gloves and belts.
CHAMPION
HEAVYWEIGHT
GLOVES
TROPHYS
THE PRIZEFIGHTER NEEDED TO GET HIS POSSESSIONS READY TO BE MOVED, SO HE ---

Now arrange the circled letters to form the surprise answer, as suggested by the above cartoon.

Print answer here

JUMBLE®

Unscramble these four Jumbles, one letter to each square, to form four ordinary words.

VAWEE

MERFA

CREMIT

CINTEF

SANDMAN BEDS
Do you have one a little harder?
We have a wide selection.
WHEN ASKED IF THEY HAD MATTRESSES THAT WEREN'T SO SOFT, THE SALESMAN SAID ---

Now arrange the circled letters to form the surprise answer, as suggested by the above cartoon.

Print answer here

JUMBLE®

Unscramble these four Jumbles, one letter to each square, to form four ordinary words.

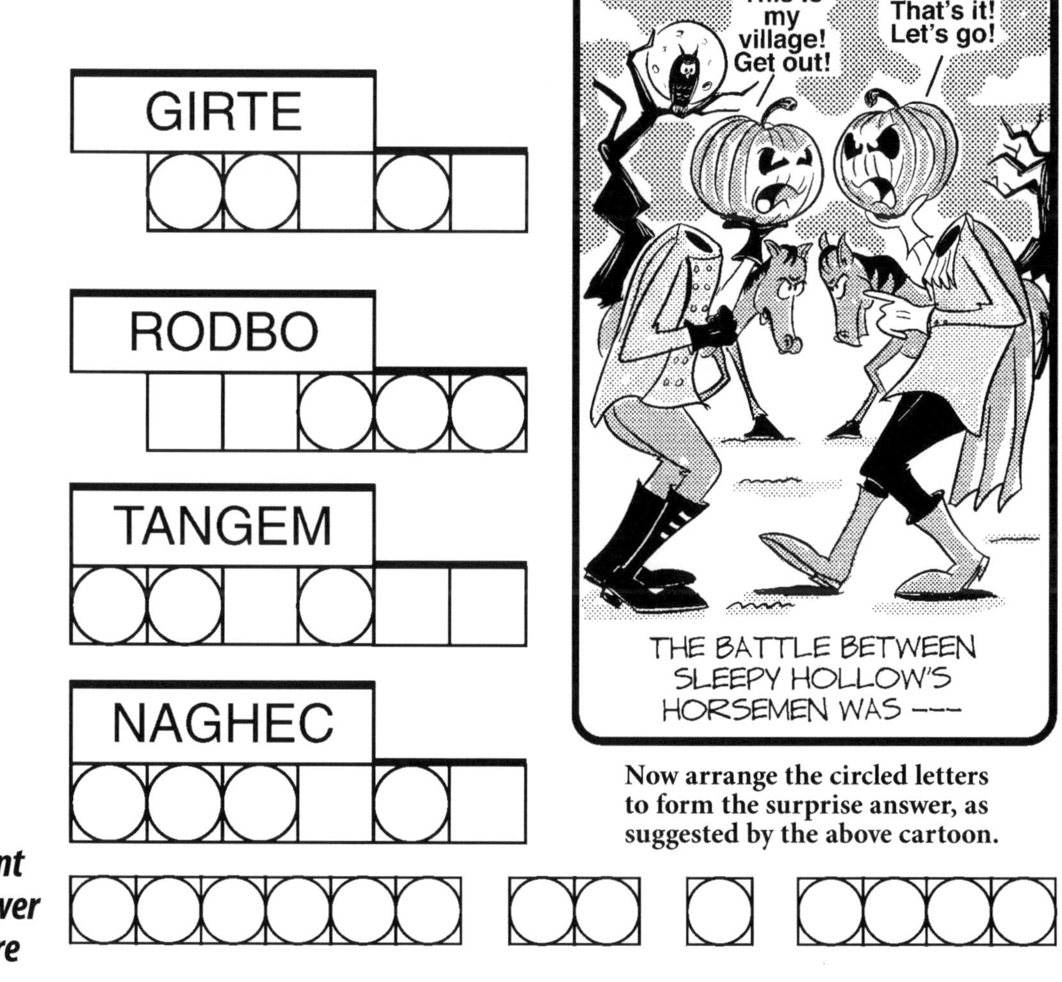
GIRTE
RODBO
TANGEM
NAGHEC
This is my village! Get out!
That's it! Let's go!
THE BATTLE BETWEEN SLEEPY HOLLOW'S HORSEMEN WAS ---

Now arrange the circled letters to form the surprise answer, as suggested by the above cartoon.

Print answer here

JUMBLE®

Unscramble these four Jumbles, one letter to each square, to form four ordinary words.

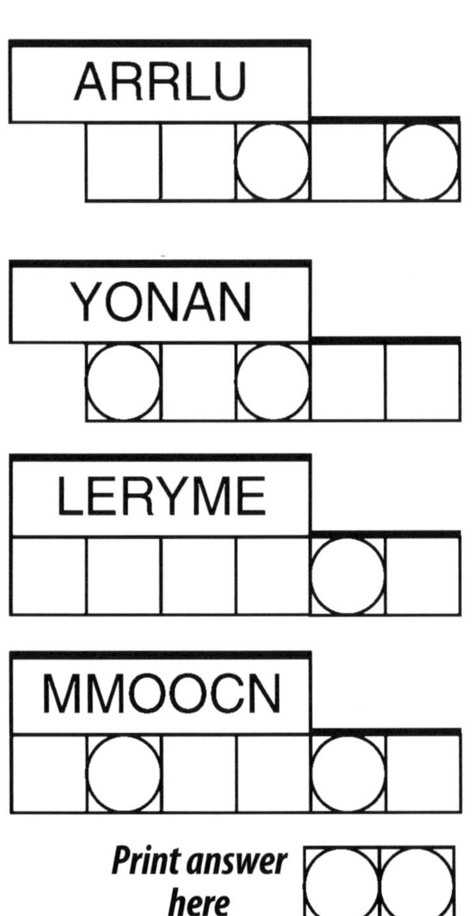
ARRLU
YONAN
LERYME
MMOOCN

BEST BUNS In TOW
People just can't get enough of these.
I'll keep them coming!
Two on sesame buns, please.
AFTER PUTTING SESAME SEEDS ON HAMBURGER BUNS, HIS BUSINESS WAS ---

Now arrange the circled letters to form the surprise answer, as suggested by the above cartoon.

Print answer here  

JUMBLE®

Unscramble these four Jumbles, one letter to each square, to form four ordinary words.

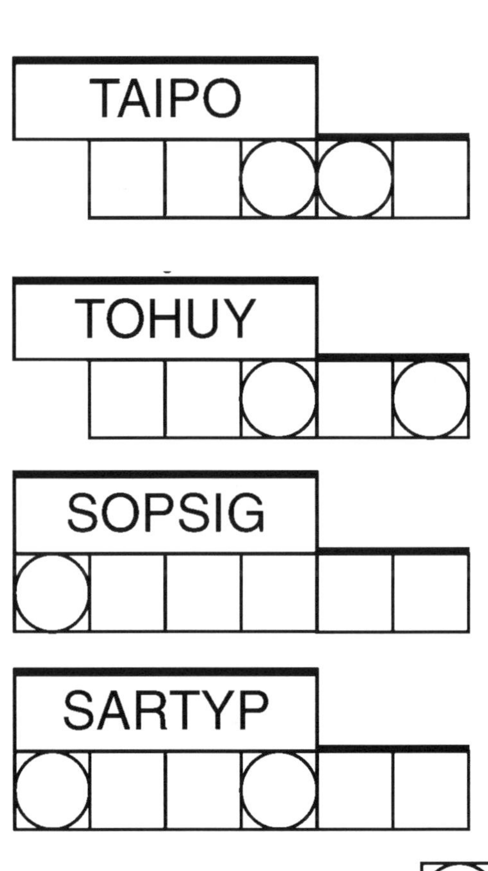
TAIPO
TOHUY
SOPSIG
SARTYP

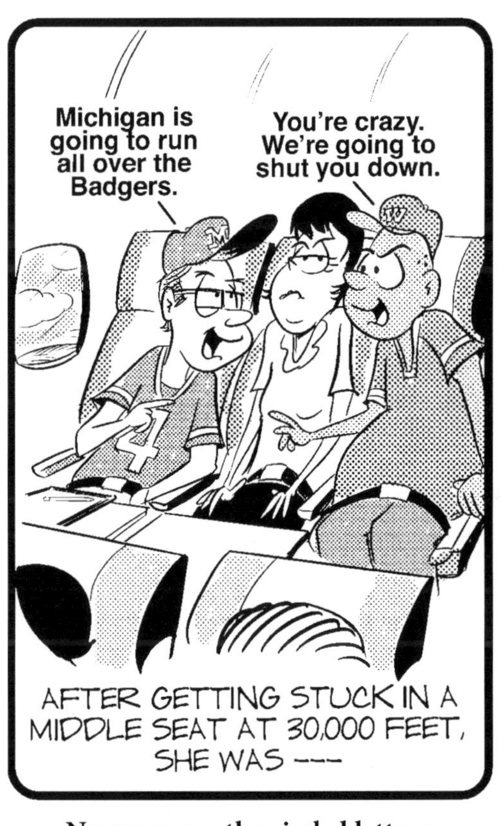
Michigan is going to run all over the Badgers.
You're crazy. We're going to shut you down.
AFTER GETTING STUCK IN A MIDDLE SEAT AT 30,000 FEET, SHE WAS ---

Now arrange the circled letters to form the surprise answer, as suggested by the above cartoon.

Print answer here

JUMBLE®

Unscramble these four Jumbles, one letter to each square, to form four ordinary words.

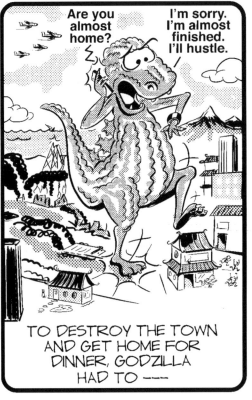

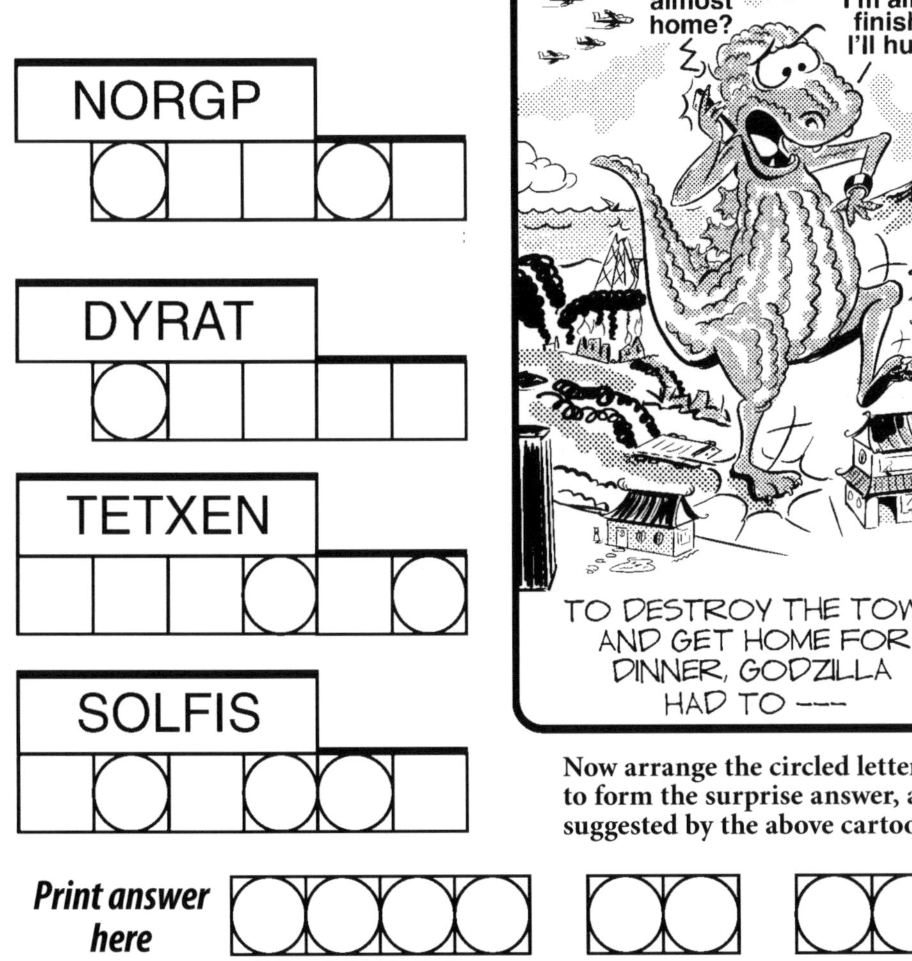
NORGP
DYRAT
TETXEN
SOLFIS
Are you almost home?
I'm sorry. I'm almost finished. I'll hustle.
TO DESTROY THE TOWN AND GET HOME FOR DINNER, GODZILLA HAD TO ---
Print answer here

Now arrange the circled letters to form the surprise answer, as suggested by the above cartoon.

JUMBLE®

Unscramble these four Jumbles, one letter to each square, to form four ordinary words.

LORTL
LITUQ
FILRAY
GEELLA
This report says the U.S. produces 200 million tons of trash annually.
Is that exactly what the report says?
WHEN HE SAID THE U.S. PRODUCES 200 MILLION TONS OF TRASH ANNUALLY, HE MEANT IT ---

Now arrange the circled letters to form the surprise answer, as suggested by the above cartoon.

Print answer here " - "

JUMBLE®

Unscramble these four Jumbles, one letter to each square, to form four ordinary words.

SERDS
OTFAO
ROLISA
PEGIMA
Did you really think this wouldn't scare him?
I thought he liked clowns.
WHEN ASKED IF THE HORROR FILM WAS TOO SCARY FOR HIS LITTLE BROTHER, HE SAID ---

Now arrange the circled letters to form the surprise answer, as suggested by the above cartoon.

Print answer here ◯'◯ ◯◯◯◯◯◯ ◯◯

JUMBLE®

Unscramble these four Jumbles, one letter to each square, to form four ordinary words.

GAEIL
RODPO
MYLOBS
NOHHOC
Round round get around
I get around
Yeah...
They sing so well together.
Their tickets were expensive, but worth every penny.
THE POPULAR CHOIR WAS PAID TO PERFORM AROUND THE WORLD AND MADE ---

Now arrange the circled letters to form the surprise answer, as suggested by the above cartoon.

Print answer here " - "

PUZZLE **126**

JUMBLE®

Unscramble these four Jumbles, one letter to each square, to form four ordinary words.

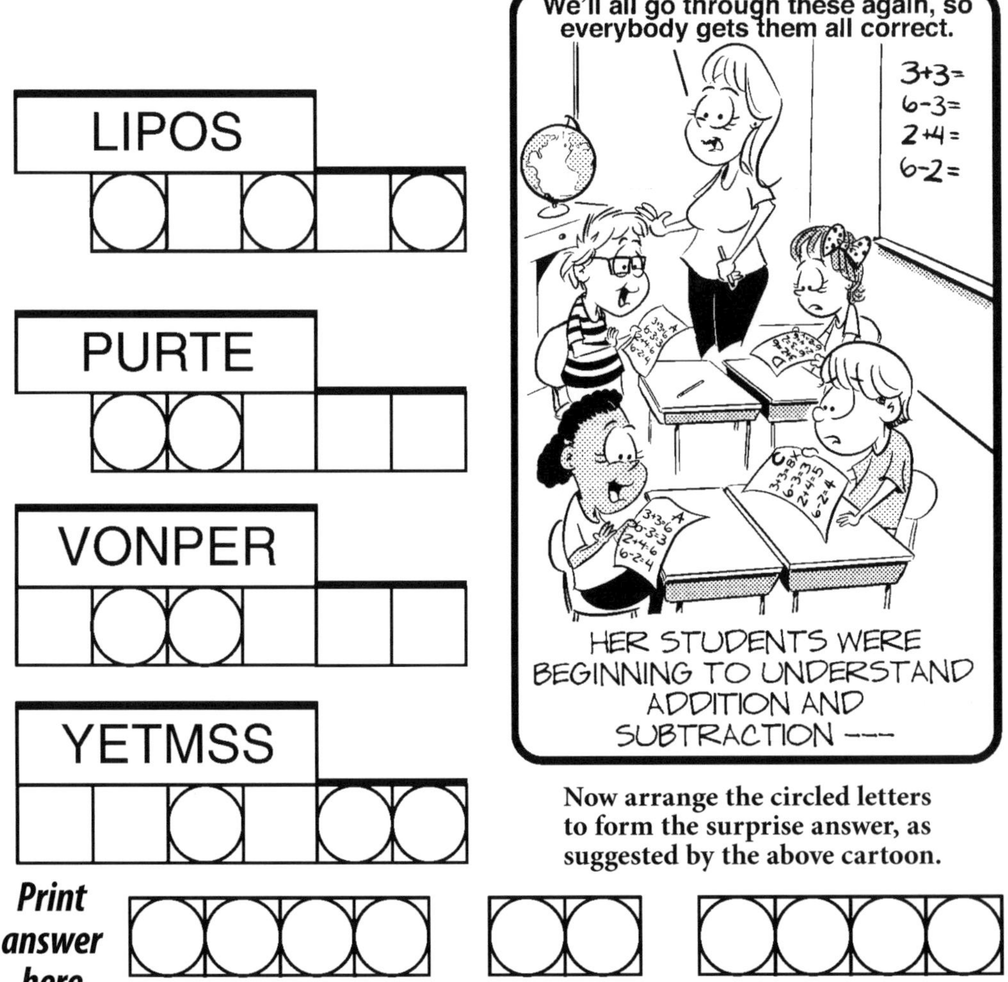
LIPOS
PURTE
VONPER
YETMSS
We'll all go through these again, so everybody gets them all correct.
3+3=
6-3=
2+4=
6-2=
HER STUDENTS WERE BEGINNING TO UNDERSTAND ADDITION AND SUBTRACTION ---

Now arrange the circled letters to form the surprise answer, as suggested by the above cartoon.

Print answer here

JUMBLE®

Unscramble these four Jumbles, one letter to each square, to form four ordinary words.

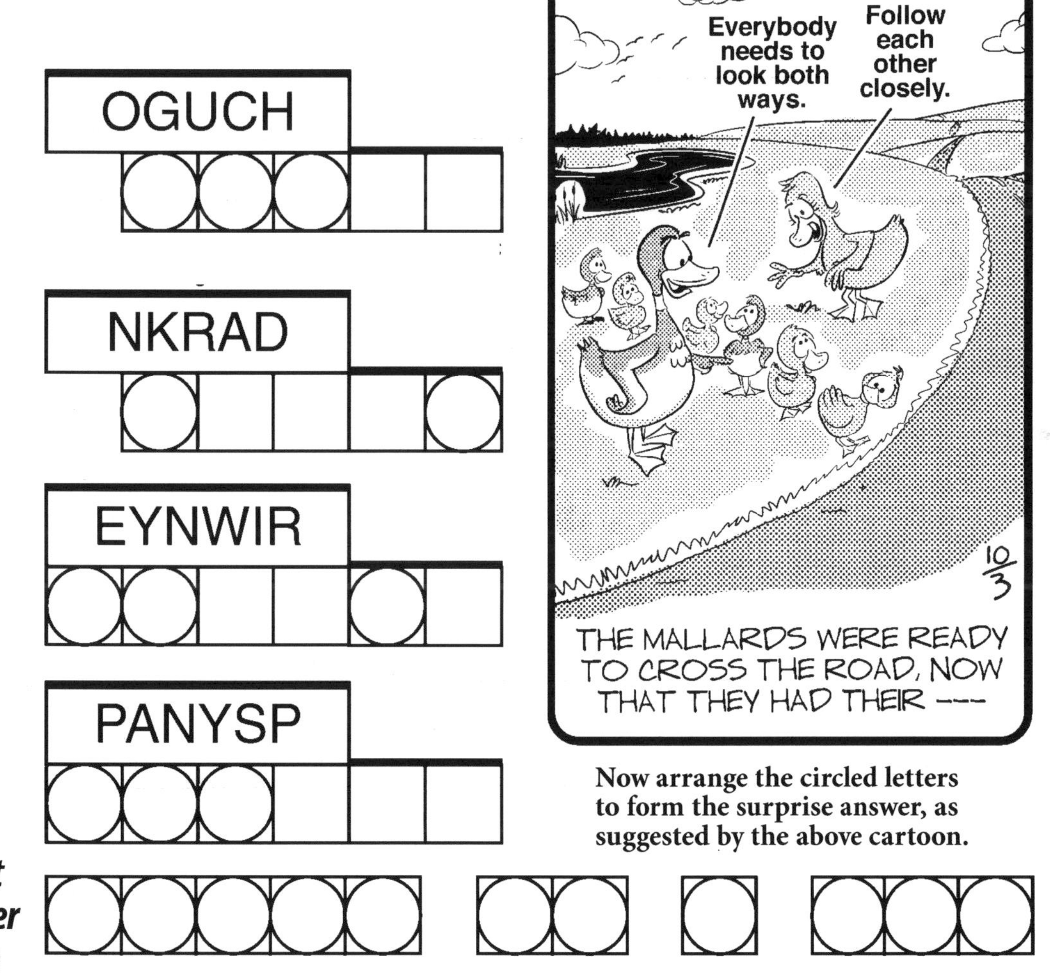

OGUCH
NKRAD
EYNWIR
PANYSP
Everybody needs to look both ways.
Follow each other closely.
10/3
THE MALLARDS WERE READY TO CROSS THE ROAD, NOW THAT THEY HAD THEIR ---

Now arrange the circled letters to form the surprise answer, as suggested by the above cartoon.

Print answer here

JUMBLE®

Unscramble these four Jumbles, one letter to each square, to form four ordinary words.

NIFAT
TYLUR
CNERDH
MAREYD
This really fits like a glove!
We want each one to be perfect.
THE FIRST BASEBALL GLOVES WERE ---
Now arrange the circled letters to form the surprise answer, as suggested by the above cartoon.
Print answer here

JUMBLE®

Unscramble these four Jumbles, one letter to each square, to form four ordinary words.

NORPG
NUYFN
ONNDEU
UDOMIP
He drives the nails with just one strike!
He's way faster than Bubba.
THOUGH SMALLER, THE CARPENTER WAS BETTER THAN HIS LARGER CO-WORKER ---

Now arrange the circled letters to form the surprise answer, as suggested by the above cartoon.

Print answer here

JUMBLE®

Unscramble these four Jumbles, one letter to each square, to form four ordinary words.

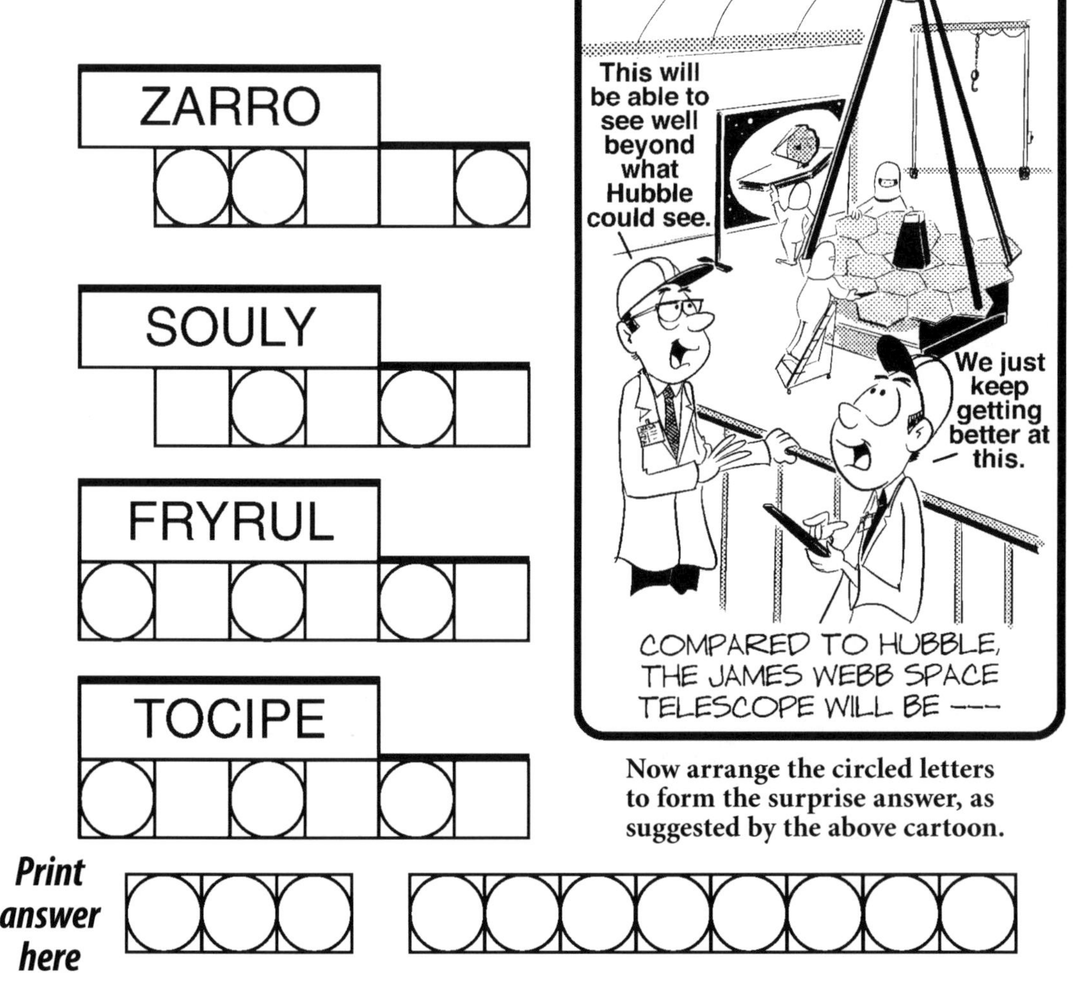

ZARRO
SOULY
FRYRUL
TOCIPE
This will be able to see well beyond what Hubble could see.
We just keep getting better at this.
COMPARED TO HUBBLE, THE JAMES WEBB SPACE TELESCOPE WILL BE ---

Now arrange the circled letters to form the surprise answer, as suggested by the above cartoon.

Print answer here

JUMBLE®

Unscramble these four Jumbles, one letter to each square, to form four ordinary words.

CORCU
NACIB
LUPARL
KAYLEW
Ha! You missed me.
That's all right. I'll be on top of my game tomorrow.
Today is not your day.
THE TIGER LEAPT AT HIS PREY, BUT MISSED. HE WAS BUMMED, BUT HE'D ----
Print answer here

Now arrange the circled letters to form the surprise answer, as suggested by the above cartoon.

JUMBLE®

Unscramble these four Jumbles, one letter to each square, to form four ordinary words.

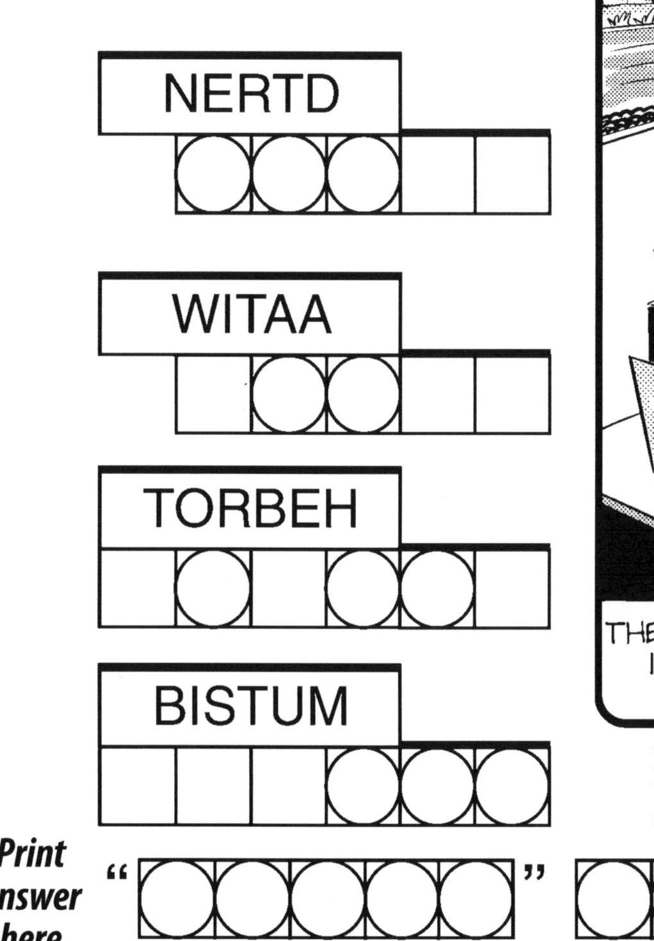
NERTD
WITAA
TORBEH
BISTUM
Print answer here

Mommy, can you cut up some grapes for me?
Let me finish this paragraph and I'll meet you in the kitchen.
THE AUTHOR LOVED WORKING IN HER BASEMENT OFFICE WHERE SHE FELT ---

Now arrange the circled letters to form the surprise answer, as suggested by the above cartoon.

“”  

JUMBLE®

Unscramble these four Jumbles, one letter to each square, to form four ordinary words.

SATTY
SEYMS
PAWYSM
PETCAC
WANTED
I thought we called someone to take care of this.
I'll call again.
WHEN THE POLICE STATION BECAME INFESTED WITH FLIES, THEY BROUGHT IN A ---

Now arrange the circled letters to form the surprise answer, as suggested by the above cartoon.

Print answer here

JUMBLE®

Unscramble these four Jumbles, one letter to each square, to form four ordinary words.

CIVEO

LITUP

REBNOK

CISETB

We need to know for certain what your blood type is for the transfusion.
I know for sure. You always have it in stock.
WHEN ASKED WHAT YOUR BLOOD TYPE IS, SOMETIMES YOU NEED TO ---

Now arrange the circled letters to form the surprise answer, as suggested by the above cartoon.

Print answer here

JUMBLE®

Unscramble these four Jumbles, one letter to each square, to form four ordinary words.

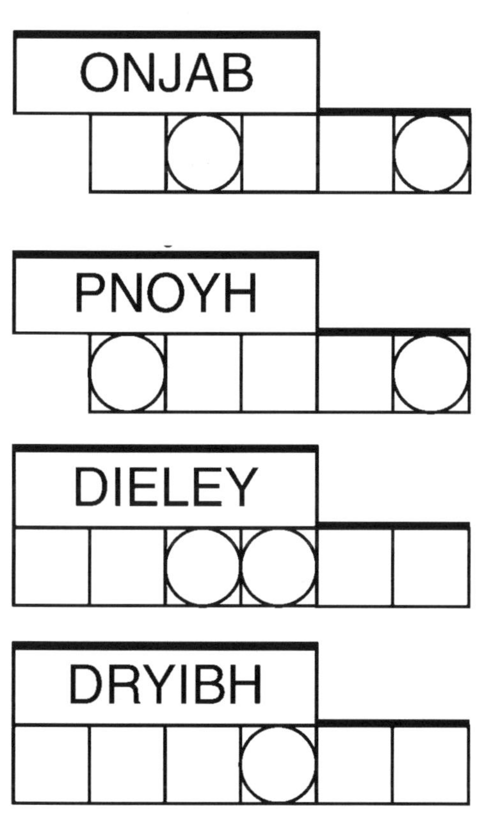
ONJAB
PNOYH
DIELEY
DRYIBH

Who loves you? I just got you the lead part in the new Jumble play.
I can't believe it! Finally, steady work.
THE ACTRESS WAS EXCITED TO GET THE PART IN THE PLAY. SHE WAS FINALLY ON THE ---

Now arrange the circled letters to form the surprise answer, as suggested by the above cartoon.

Print answer here "◯◯◯-◯◯◯◯"

JUMBLE®

Unscramble these four Jumbles, one letter to each square, to form four ordinary words.

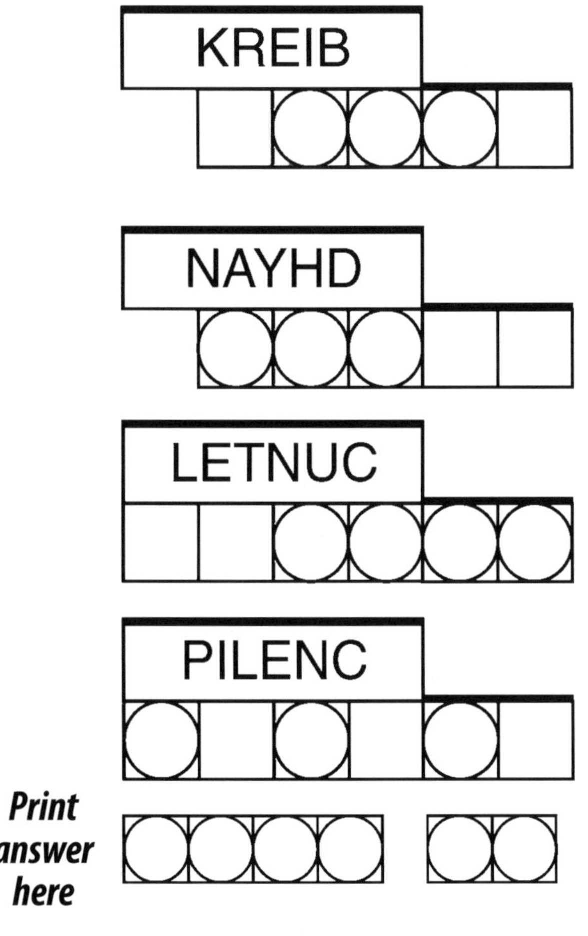
KREIB
NAYHD
LETNUC
PILENC

You have the most beautiful eyes.
My eyes are up here.
You're so irritating.
SHE ASKED THE OBNOXIOUS VAMPIRE TO LEAVE HER ALONE WHEN HE BECAME A ---

Now arrange the circled letters to form the surprise answer, as suggested by the above cartoon.

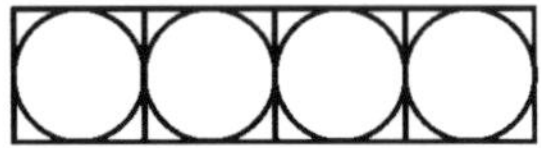

Print answer here

JUMBLE®

Unscramble these four Jumbles, one letter to each square, to form four ordinary words.

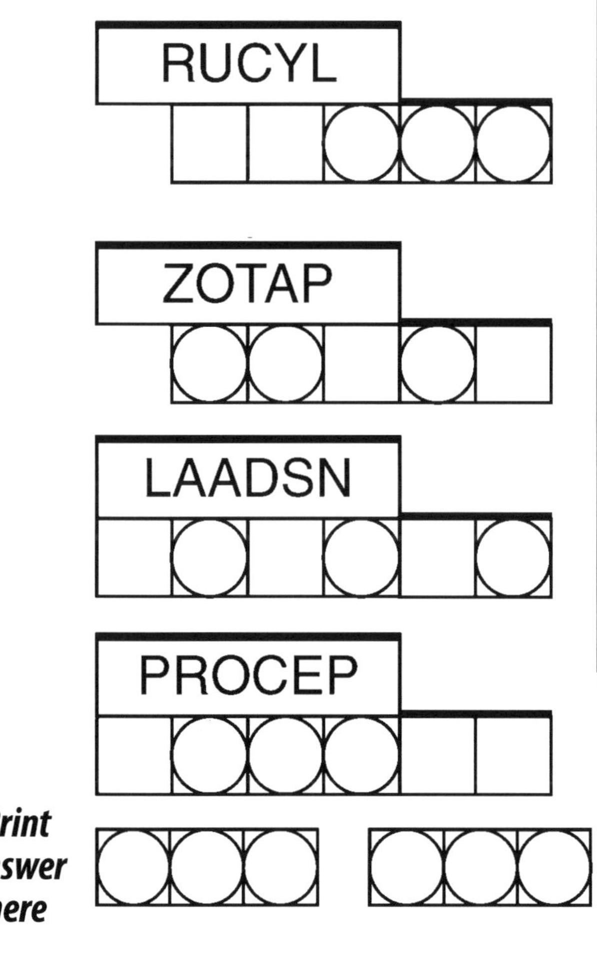
RUCYL
ZOTAP
LAADSN
PROCEP

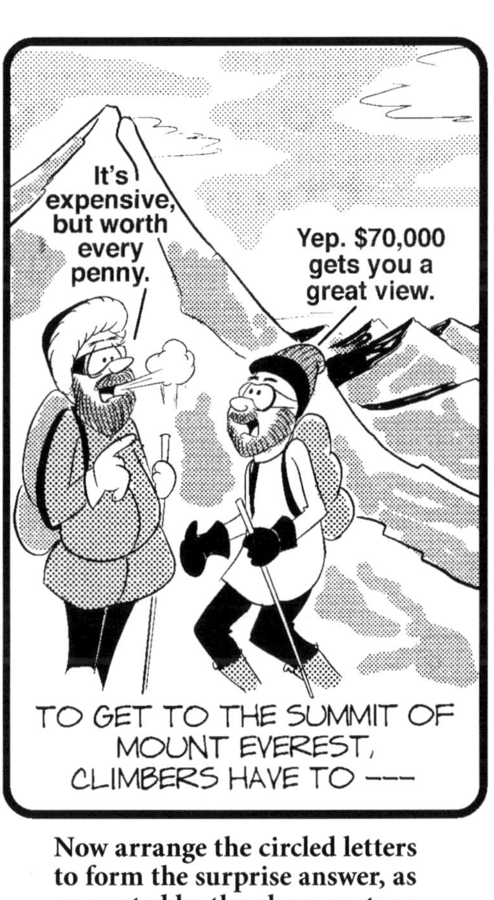
It's expensive, but worth every penny.
Yep. $70,000 gets you a great view.
TO GET TO THE SUMMIT OF MOUNT EVEREST, CLIMBERS HAVE TO ---

Now arrange the circled letters to form the surprise answer, as suggested by the above cartoon.

Print answer here

JUMBLE®

Unscramble these four Jumbles, one letter to each square, to form four ordinary words.

CARTT
JEYON
FELUEY
ROVYAS
All done.
Wow! First again. You're cruising through this course.
SPEED READING 101
THE BEST STUDENT IN THE SPEED-READING CLASS WAS A ---

Now arrange the circled letters to form the surprise answer, as suggested by the above cartoon.

Print answer here

JUMBLE®

Unscramble these four Jumbles, one letter to each square, to form four ordinary words.

DORED
WLONC
TIMERP
SOOURP
It's only been used once. And it's all yours at 90 percent off.
Is this a shark bite?
Does it even work?
90% OFF
THEY BECAME SKEPTICAL OF THE SCUBA EQUIPMENT AFTER SEEING THE ---
Print answer here

Now arrange the circled letters to form the surprise answer, as suggested by the above cartoon.

JUMBLE®

Unscramble these four Jumbles, one letter to each square, to form four ordinary words.

GANYT
XTREE
BLUMME
UNSOIC
They are both synchronized to the atomic clock.
Let's buy them!
4:00
THE TWINS BOUGHT IDENTICAL WRISTWATCHES AT THE ---

Now arrange the circled letters to form the surprise answer, as suggested by the above cartoon.

Print answer here

JUMBLE®

Unscramble these four Jumbles, one letter to each square, to form four ordinary words.

DUEGN

NERDT

NINBUO

MUURQO

Overall, you did great. Let's work on those you missed.
8-A
2-B
2-C
0-D
0-F
THE TEACHER WAS HAPPY THAT THOSE WHO DID POORLY ON THE MATH TEST WERE ---

Now arrange the circled letters to form the surprise answer, as suggested by the above cartoon.

Print answer here

JUMBLE®

Unscramble these four Jumbles, one letter to each square, to form four ordinary words.

JOTSI
LEERD
WLOOLH
ENISCC
Perfect timing!
Here are the gems!
THE DELIVERY OF DIAMONDS, RUBIES AND EMERALDS ARRIVED AT THE STORE ---

Now arrange the circled letters to form the surprise answer, as suggested by the above cartoon.

Print answer here ◯◯ "◯◯◯◯◯-◯◯◯◯◯"

JUMBLE®

Unscramble these four Jumbles, one letter to each square, to form four ordinary words.

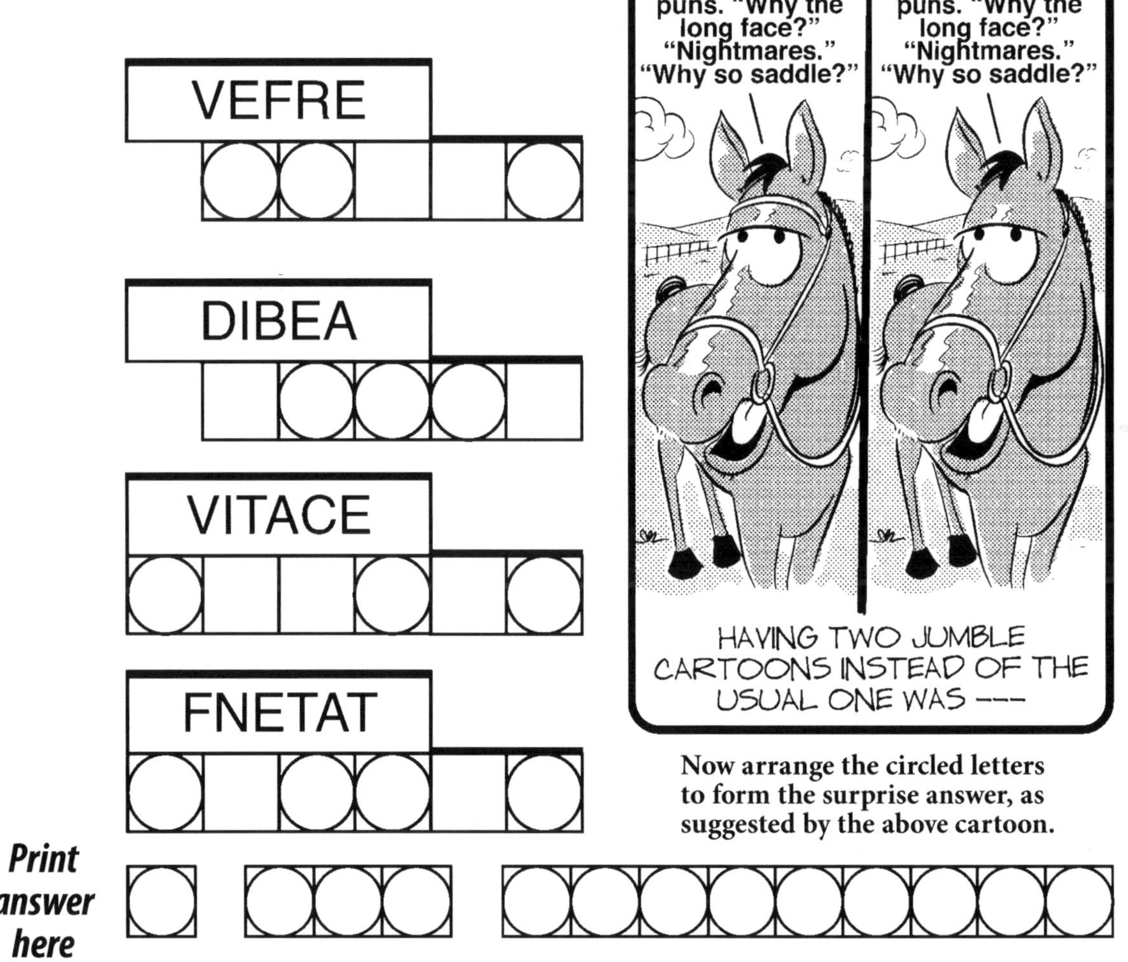
VEFRE
DIBEA
VITACE
FNETAT
I've heard your puns. "Why the long face?" "Nightmares." "Why so saddle?"
I've heard your puns. "Why the long face?" "Nightmares." "Why so saddle?"
HAVING TWO JUMBLE CARTOONS INSTEAD OF THE USUAL ONE WAS ---

Now arrange the circled letters to form the surprise answer, as suggested by the above cartoon.

Print answer here

JUMBLE®

Unscramble these four Jumbles, one letter to each square, to form four ordinary words.

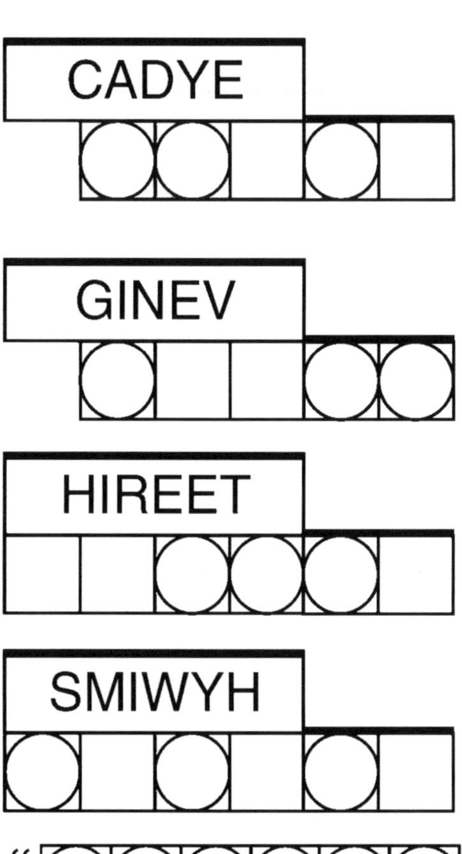
CADYE
GINEV
HIREET
SMIWYH

I want to be Mr. Universe someday.
Just keep pumping up, Arnold.
Be patient. It may take a while.
WOULD HE BECOME A PROFESSIONAL BODYBUILDER? HE'D HAVE TO —

Now arrange the circled letters to form the surprise answer, as suggested by the above cartoon.

Print answer here

“”  

JUMBLE®

Unscramble these four Jumbles, one letter to each square, to form four ordinary words.

So, what do you think?
You really know what you're doing.
WHEN THEY FINISHED DRILLING FOR WATER, THE OWNER OF THE PROPERTY SAID ---

ZOWYO

VONLE

OYENLL

LIVDER

Now arrange the circled letters to form the surprise answer, as suggested by the above cartoon.

Print answer here

JUMBLE®

Unscramble these four Jumbles, one letter to each square, to form four ordinary words.

LOCTU

EELPO

DARTNS

IONLIV

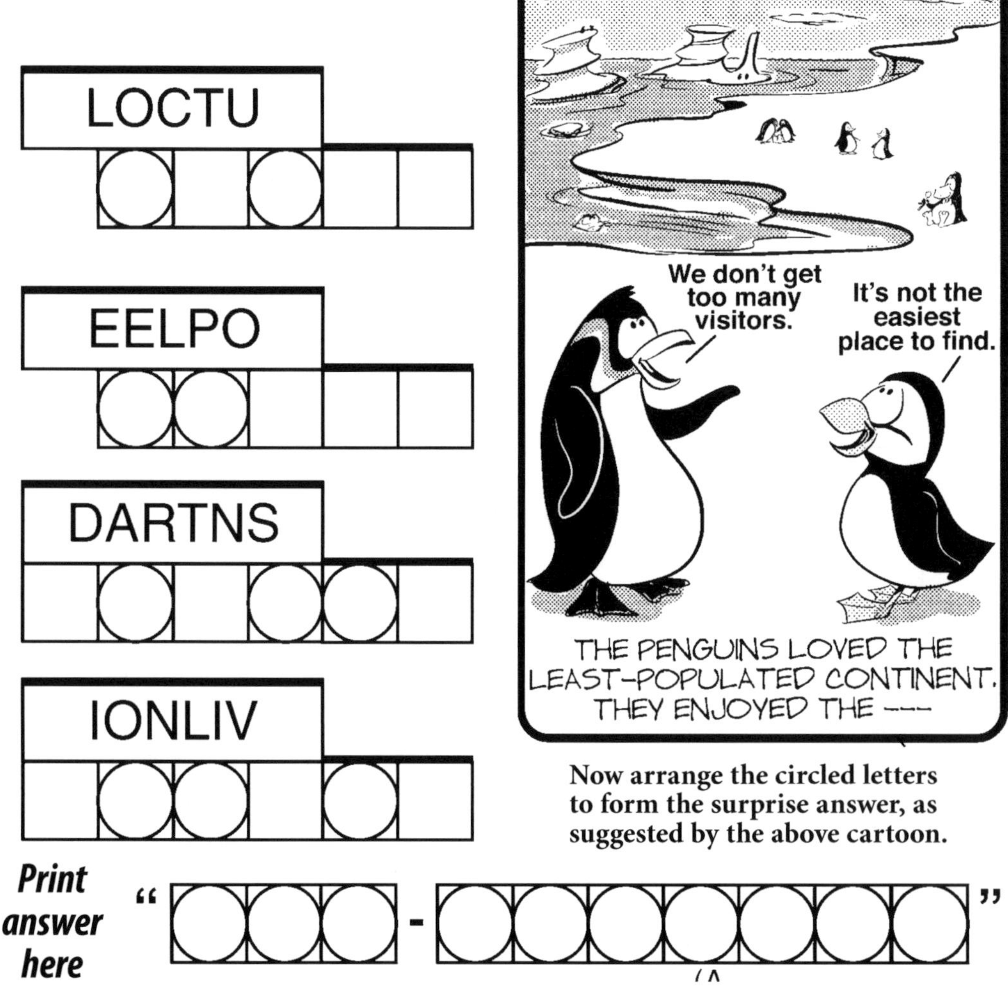
We don't get too many visitors.
It's not the easiest place to find.
THE PENGUINS LOVED THE LEAST-POPULATED CONTINENT. THEY ENJOYED THE ---

Now arrange the circled letters to form the surprise answer, as suggested by the above cartoon.

Print answer here " - "

JUMBLE®

Unscramble these four Jumbles, one letter to each square, to form four ordinary words.

RALAV

IBCAS

DINDEH

SKNIRH

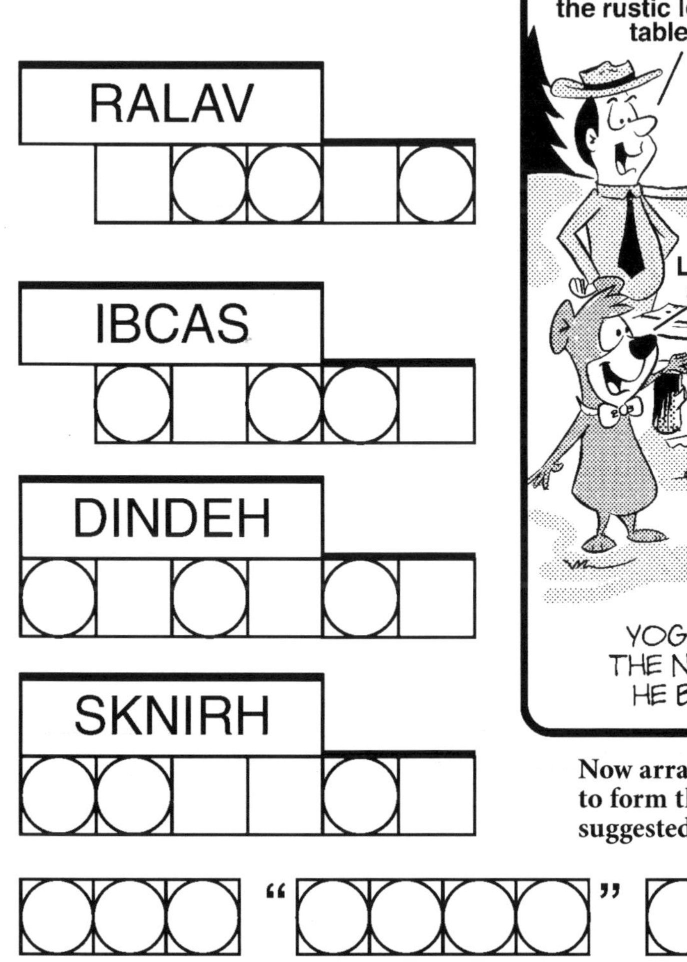
Well, this is quite the rustic looking table.
It's better than your average table.
Let's have a picnic, Yogi.
YOGI SHOWED OFF THE NEW TABLE THAT HE BUILT WITH ----

Now arrange the circled letters to form the surprise answer, as suggested by the above cartoon.

Print answer here ◯◯◯ "◯◯◯◯" ◯◯◯◯◯

JUMBLE®

Unscramble these four Jumbles, one letter to each square, to form four ordinary words.

RIVEP

SIDAY

PCLUTS

LERYAN

I love all the food choices here.
P.S. BANGKOK 2
MANNY'S D
THEY MOVED TO AN AREA WITH MANY DIFFERENT TYPES OF PEOPLE. THEY LOVED THE ---

Now arrange the circled letters to form the surprise answer, as suggested by the above cartoon.

Print answer here " - "

JUMBLE®

Unscramble these four Jumbles, one letter to each square, to form four ordinary words.

OLTAT
SERHF
FLYSME
LAVEBI
What was it like winning these medals?
It was amazing. I took a tenth of a second off in London and another in Paris.
9.82
9.92
WHEN THE RETIRED SPRINTER TALKED ABOUT HIS RECORDS, HE RECALLED THE ---

Now arrange the circled letters to form the surprise answer, as suggested by the above cartoon.

Print answer here

JUMBLE®

Unscramble these four Jumbles, one letter to each square, to form four ordinary words.

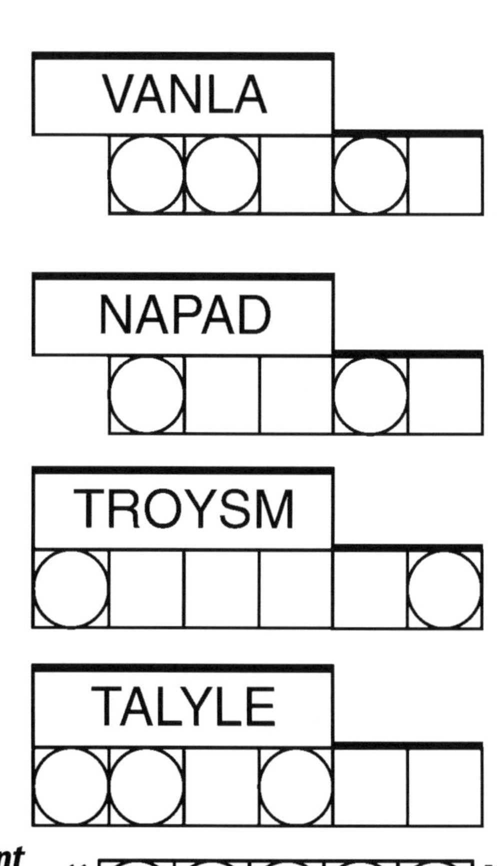
VANLA
NAPAD
TROYSM
TALYLE

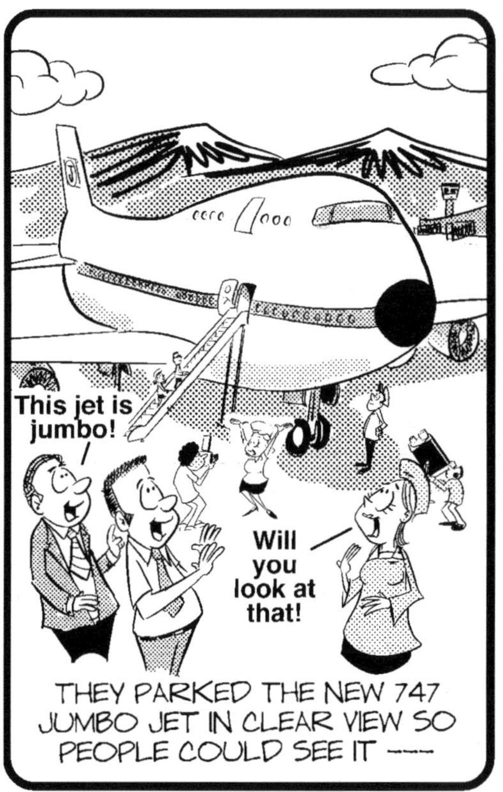
This jet is jumbo!
Will you look at that!
THEY PARKED THE NEW 747 JUMBO JET IN CLEAR VIEW SO PEOPLE COULD SEE IT ---

Now arrange the circled letters to form the surprise answer, as suggested by the above cartoon.

Print answer here " "  

JUMBLE®

Unscramble these four Jumbles, one letter to each square, to form four ordinary words.

NATDS
BIREB
XLAEEH
ORUPTO
I can't wait to master judo like I did karate.
Well, until you do, you'll need this color.
THE MARTIAL ARTS MASTER STARTING LEARNING JUDO BECAUSE HE HAD KARATE ---

Now arrange the circled letters to form the surprise answer, as suggested by the above cartoon.

Print answer here

JUMBLE®

Unscramble these four Jumbles, one letter to each square, to form four ordinary words.

REAPO
GODDE
KNUHRS
MAHWRT
Your apricot jam is wonderful!
Tell your friends!
Try it on this toast
Yum, tart cherry.
TRY ME
HER CUSTOMERS LOVED HER JELLIES AND JAMS. NOW SHE HOPED THEY WOULD ---
Now arrange the circled letters to form the surprise answer, as suggested by the above cartoon.
Print answer here

JUMBLE®

Unscramble these four Jumbles, one letter to each square, to form four ordinary words.

Today's Guest JUMBLER is
MIKE PETERS
creator of MOTHER GOOSE AND GRIMM
NEDRT
ESEGE
OYPRET
GNEEDL
MIKE PETERS
?
GRIMM WANTED TO GO TO COLLEGE TO GET HIS...
Print answer here

Now arrange the circled letters to form the surprise answer, as suggested by the above cartoon.

JUMBLE®

Unscramble these four Jumbles, one letter to each square, to form four ordinary words.

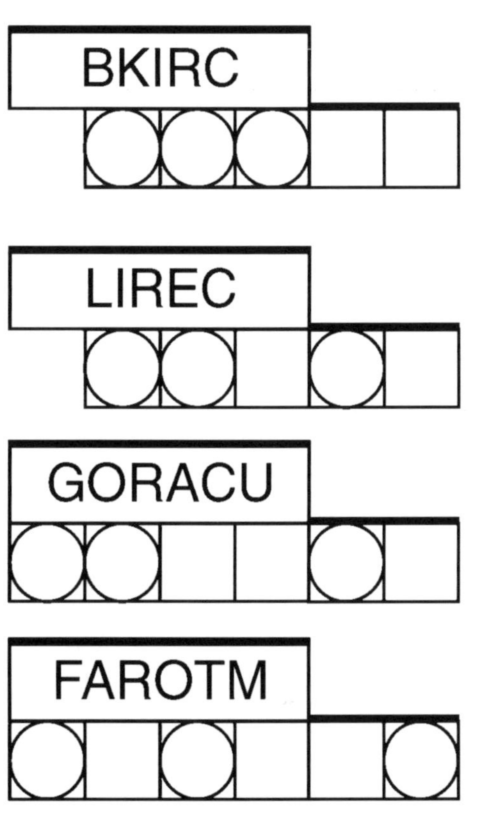
BKIRC
LIREC
GORACU
FAROTM

Today's Guest JUMBLER is
RICH POWELL
creator of WIDE OPEN!
Look, I'm no EINSWINE, but...
Take my sow, Please!
...So, I told Him I was Disgruntled!
RIB Ticklers Comedy CLUB
Yawn.
ugh.
R. Powell
Swinefeld thought he was one Fantastic Comedian, but he was really just a — —

Now arrange the circled letters to form the surprise answer, as suggested by the above cartoon.

Print answer here

JUMBLE®

Unscramble these four Jumbles, one letter to each square, to form four ordinary words.

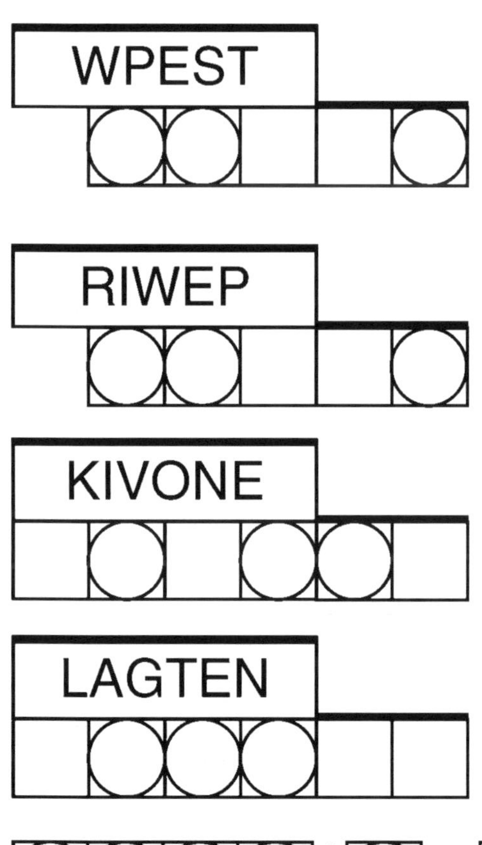
WPEST
RIWEP
KIVONE
LAGTEN

Today's Guest JUMBLERs are
Steve Kelley & Jeff Parker
creators of DUSTIN
THANKS, BUT I'M HAPPY WITH MY PRESENT POSITION.
HELP WANTED
Corn Chips
KELLEY and PARKER
HELEN AND ED'S ATTEMPT TO CONVINCE DUSTIN TO GET A JOB---

Now arrange the circled letters to form the surprise answer, as suggested by the above cartoon.

Print answer here

JUMBLE®

Unscramble these four Jumbles, one letter to each square, to form four ordinary words.

SLIBS

KIKAH

ILANFE

DIACEV

Today's Guest JUMBLER is
TERRI LIBENSON
creator of THE PAJAMA DIARIES
Libenson 11–17
You told us to cut the recipe down, so we put it in for 10 minutes at 150 degrees.
WHEN JILL ASKS HER KIDS FOR HELP WITH DINNER, THE RESULTS ARE ---

Now arrange the circled letters to form the surprise answer, as suggested by the above cartoon.

Print answer here ◯◯◯◯-◯◯◯◯◯

JUMBLE®

Unscramble these four Jumbles, one letter to each square, to form four ordinary words.

CNIAP
LEECX
POYROD
LUWANT
Today's Guest JUMBLER is
ERIC REAVES
artist for HI AND LOIS
BROWNE
FALLING ASLEEP IN THE SUNBEAM WITH HER SOLAR CELL TOY WAS A ---
Now arrange the circled letters to form the surprise answer, as suggested by the above cartoon.
Print answer here

JUMBLE®

Unscramble these four Jumbles, one letter to each square, to form four ordinary words.

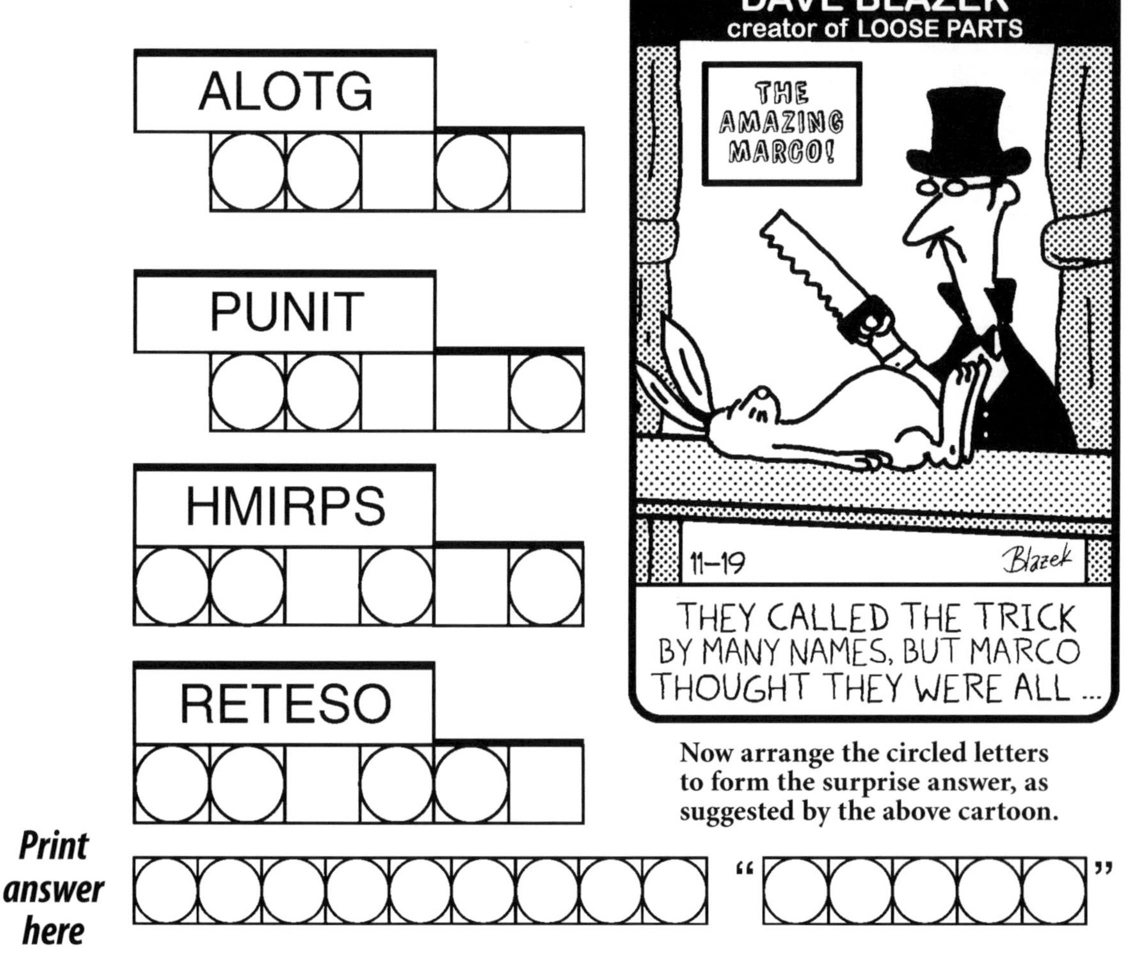
ALOTG
PUNIT
HMIRPS
RETESO
Today's Guest JUMBLER is
DAVE BLAZEK
creator of LOOSE PARTS
THE AMAZING MARCO!
11-19
Blazek
THEY CALLED THE TRICK BY MANY NAMES, BUT MARCO THOUGHT THEY WERE ALL ...

Now arrange the circled letters to form the surprise answer, as suggested by the above cartoon.

Print answer here

JUMBLE®

Unscramble these four Jumbles, one letter to each square, to form four ordinary words.

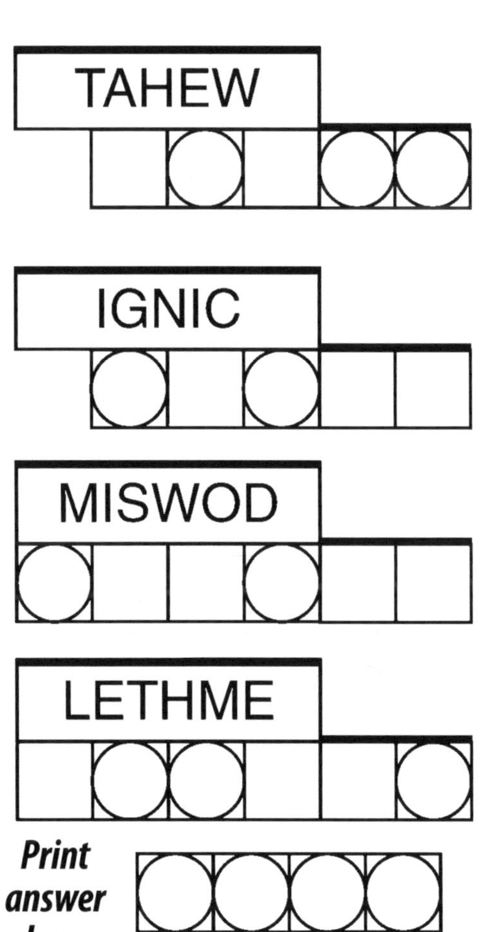
TAHEW
IGNIC
MISWOD
LETHME

What are we going to do?
I don't see any cards!
Oh, no! Gizmo ate the deck!
AFTER THE DOG RIPPED UP THE DECK OF CARDS, THE POKER PLAYERS COULDN'T ---

Now arrange the circled letters to form the surprise answer, as suggested by the above cartoon.

Print answer here

JUMBLE®

Unscramble these four Jumbles, one letter to each square, to form four ordinary words.

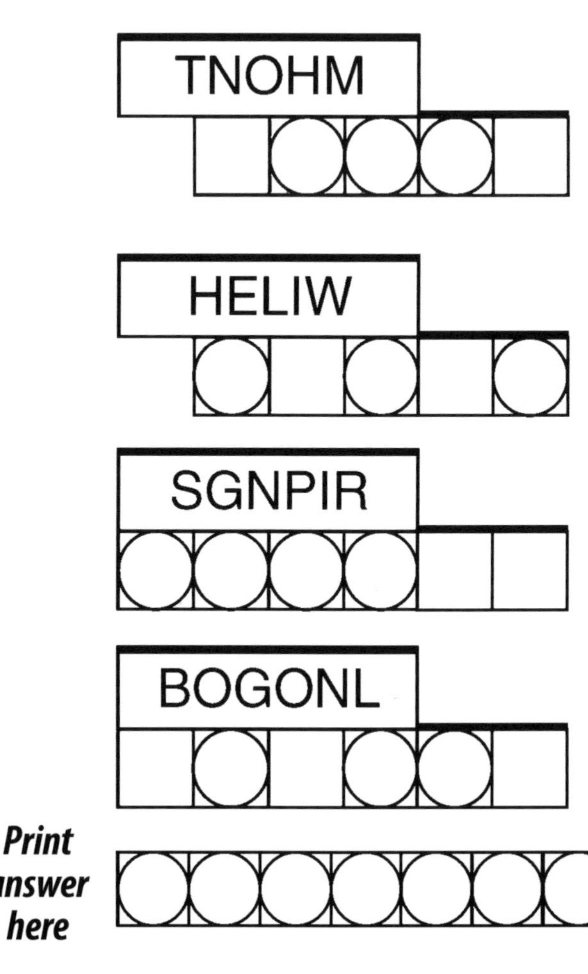
TNOHM
HELIW
SGNPIR
BOGONL

I thought you girls might like a little treat.
These are the best!
Way better than cookies.
Yum!
WHEN SHE BROUGHT THE GIRLS DELICIOUS CAKE-LIKE COOKIES, SHE EARNED ---

Now arrange the circled letters to form the surprise answer, as suggested by the above cartoon.

Print answer here

JUMBLE®
Neighbor

Challenger Puzzles

JUMBLE®

Unscramble these six Jumbles, one letter to each square, to form six ordinary words.

NEEVEL
PLARIL
ANNAAB
EGMAIP
INLOIV
GLIMYR
DID ALL THAT TROUBLE IN THE GARDEN OF EDEN INVOLVE A RED APPLE?

Now arrange the circled letters to form the surprise answer, as suggested by the above cartoon.

Print answer here

JUMBLE®

Unscramble these six Jumbles, one letter to each square, to form six ordinary words.

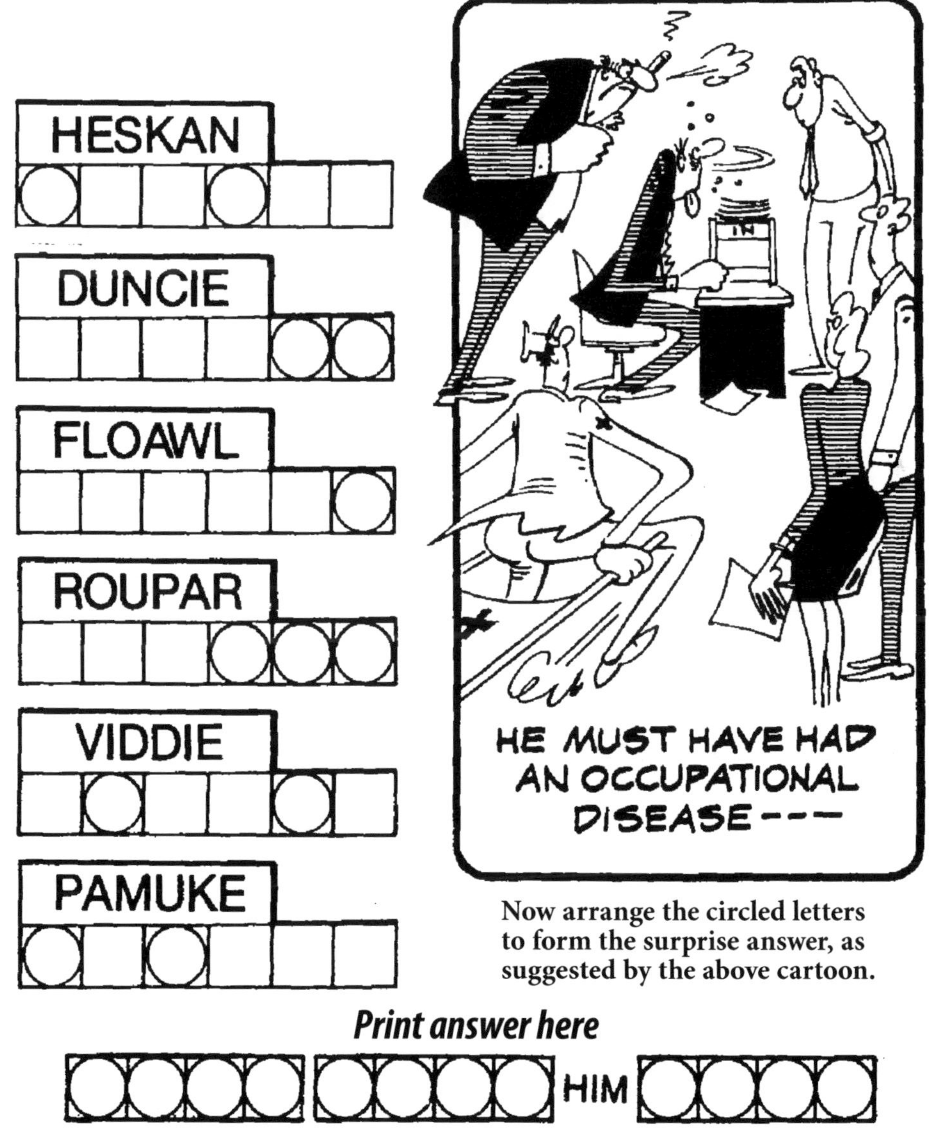
HESKAN
DUNCIE
FLOAWL
ROUPAR
VIDDIE
PAMUKE
IN
HE MUST HAVE HAD AN OCCUPATIONAL DISEASE---

Now arrange the circled letters to form the surprise answer, as suggested by the above cartoon.

Print answer here

( ) ( ) ( ) ( ) ( ) ( ) ( ) ( ) HIM ( ) ( ) ( ) ( )

JUMBLE®

Unscramble these six Jumbles, one letter to each square, to form six ordinary words.

TOESGO
FESTOF
TOALZE
GLUDEE
RUFIAN
PARAPE
HOW HE LEARNED ALL ABOUT THE BIRDS.

Now arrange the circled letters to form the surprise answer, as suggested by the above cartoon.

Print answer here

IT WAS " - "

JUMBLE®

Unscramble these six Jumbles, one letter to each square, to form six ordinary words.

CROVAT
SOXEEP
HEEBAD
ROMMIE
TANFUL
YURJIN
Mother always wanted me to follow in her footsteps
Can't wait to hang up my own shingle
WHAT KIND OF A TEST DO THEY TAKE IN ORDER TO GET A LICENSE IN WITCHCRAFT?
Now arrange the circled letters to form the surprise answer, as suggested by the above cartoon.
Print answer here
A " - "

JUMBLE®

Unscramble these six Jumbles, one letter to each square, to form six ordinary words.

BARNEY

GAZZIG

NACTAV

BOILAN

STOUBE

ONSOAL

How do you like my party?
A CORKSCREW MIGHT ALSO BE USEFUL FOR OPENING THIS.

Now arrange the circled letters to form the surprise answer, as suggested by the above cartoon.

Print answer here

A

JUMBLE®

Unscramble these six Jumbles, one letter to each square, to form six ordinary words.

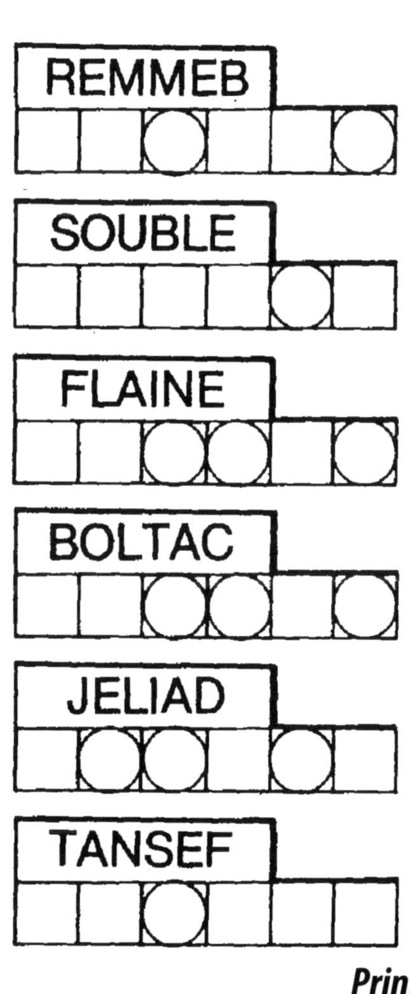
REMMEB
SOUBLE
FLAINE
BOLTAC
JELIAD
TANSEF

Makes me feel more human
WHAT STIRRUPS ARE EXPECTED TO DO.

Now arrange the circled letters to form the surprise answer, as suggested by the above cartoon.

Print answer here

ABOVE THE

JUMBLE®

Unscramble these six Jumbles, one letter to each square, to form six ordinary words.

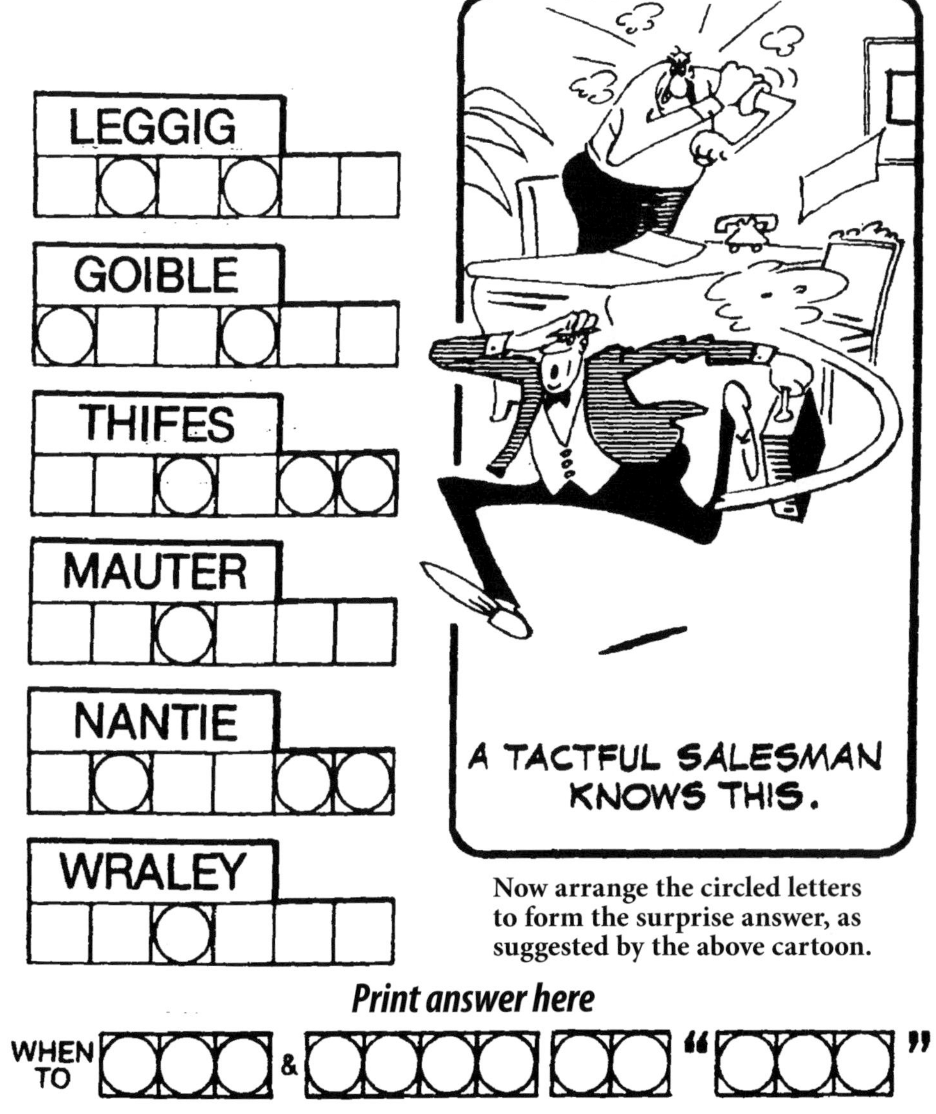
LEGGIG
GOIBLE
THIFES
MAUTER
NANTIE
WRALEY
A TACTFUL SALESMAN KNOWS THIS.
Now arrange the circled letters to form the surprise answer, as suggested by the above cartoon.
Print answer here
WHEN TO
&
“ ”

PUZZLE 168

JUMBLE®

Unscramble these six Jumbles, one letter to each square, to form six ordinary words.

LOICAS
CRANDI
DUNLOF
INGUSE
VIQUER
BLOGON
Every child needs a pet
WHAT THAT MILD-MANNERED DINOSAUR WAS.
A

Now arrange the circled letters to form the surprise answer, as suggested by the above cartoon.

Print answer here

JUMBLE®

Unscramble these six Jumbles, one letter to each square, to form six ordinary words.

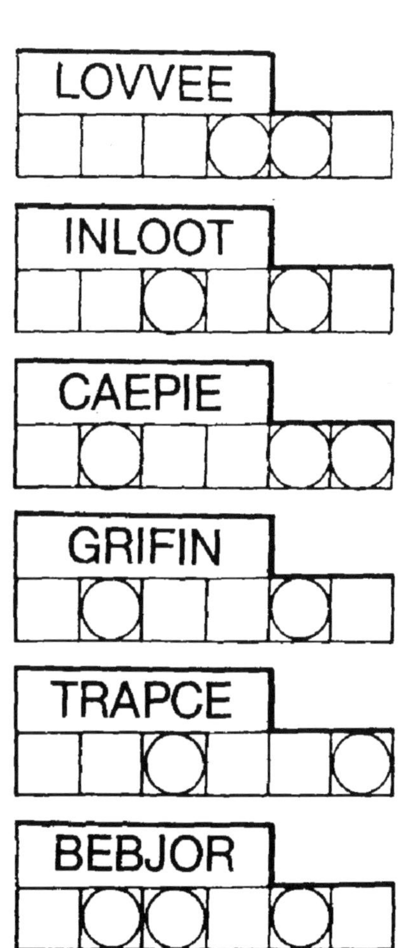
LOVVEE
INLOOT
CAEPIE
GRIFIN
TRAPCE
BEBJOR

ANOTHER NAME FOR A WIG.

Now arrange the circled letters to form the surprise answer, as suggested by the above cartoon.

Print answer here

A

JUMBLE®

Unscramble these six Jumbles, one letter to each square, to form six ordinary words.

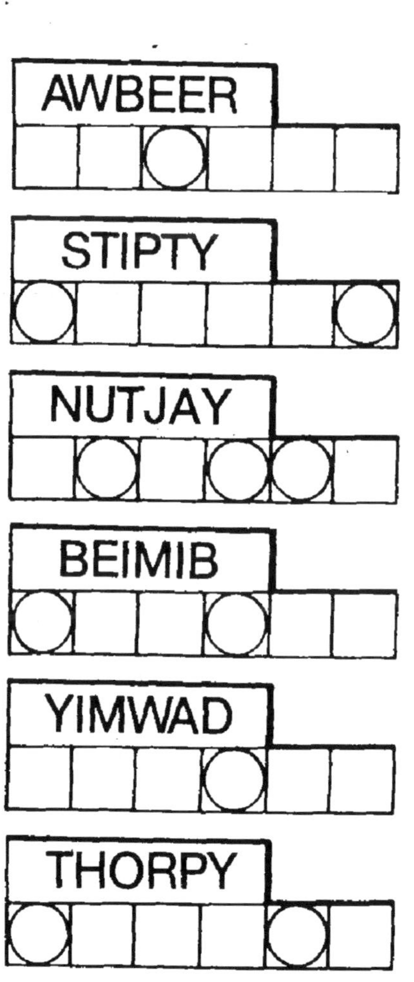
AWBEER
STIPTY
NUTJAY
BEIMIB
YIMWAD
THORPY

He thinks he's being funny
BAR
WHAT A TAUNT MIGHT BE.

Now arrange the circled letters to form the surprise answer, as suggested by the above cartoon.

Print answer here

MORE

JUMBLE®

Unscramble these six Jumbles, one letter to each square, to form six ordinary words.

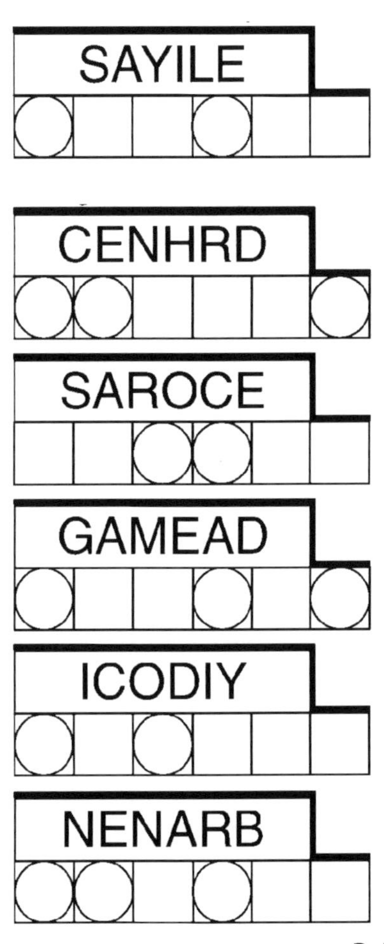
SAYILE
CENHRD
SAROCE
GAMEAD
ICODIY
NENARB

I've been trying them out on you. I think you'd look great in this one.
Are you kidding me? I'd look pretty foolish in these.
$1500
HIS WIFE WANTED HIM TO GET A TOUPEE, BUT HE THOUGHT IT WAS A ---

Now arrange the circled letters to form the surprise answer, as suggested by the above cartoon.

Print answer here

JUMBLE®

Unscramble these six Jumbles, one letter to each square, to form six ordinary words.

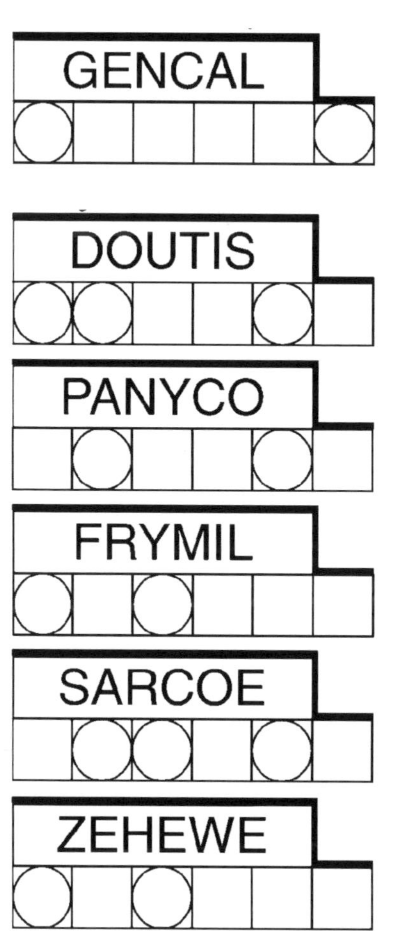
GENCAL
DOUTIS
PANYCO
FRYMIL
SARCOE
ZEHEWE

Best-selling authors may wear the Writer's Robe.
Welcome to our society. It is time to sign the book.
Ooh, the Quote Quill! I've heard about this.
WHEN THE YOUNG AUTHOR SOLD HIS FIRST BOOK, HE AND OTHER AUTHORS CELEBRATED HIS ---

Now arrange the circled letters to form the surprise answer, as suggested by the above cartoon.

Print answer here

JUMBLE®

Unscramble these six Jumbles, one letter to each square, to form six ordinary words.

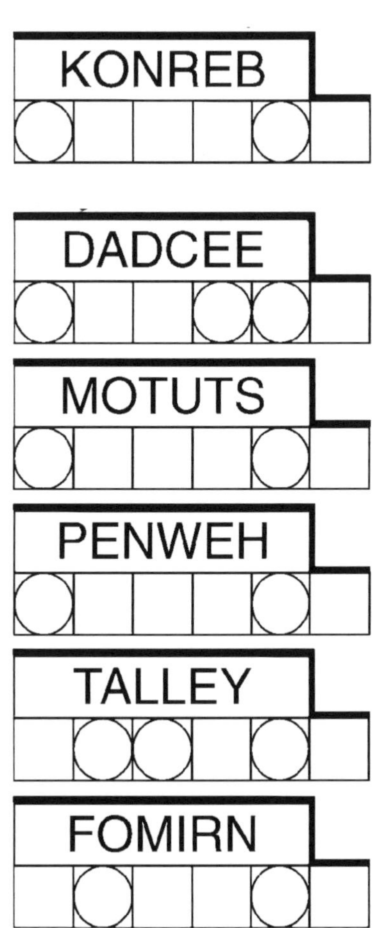
KONREB
DADCEE
MOTUTS
PENWEH
TALLEY
FOMIRN

Space and time should be considered together and in relation to each other.
I'm sorry. Why is this relative?
E=mc²
NOT FULLY COMPREHENDING EINSTEIN'S GENERAL THEORY OF RELATIVITY WAS ---

Now arrange the circled letters to form the surprise answer, as suggested by the above cartoon.

Print answer here

JUMBLE®

Unscramble these six Jumbles, one letter to each square, to form six ordinary words.

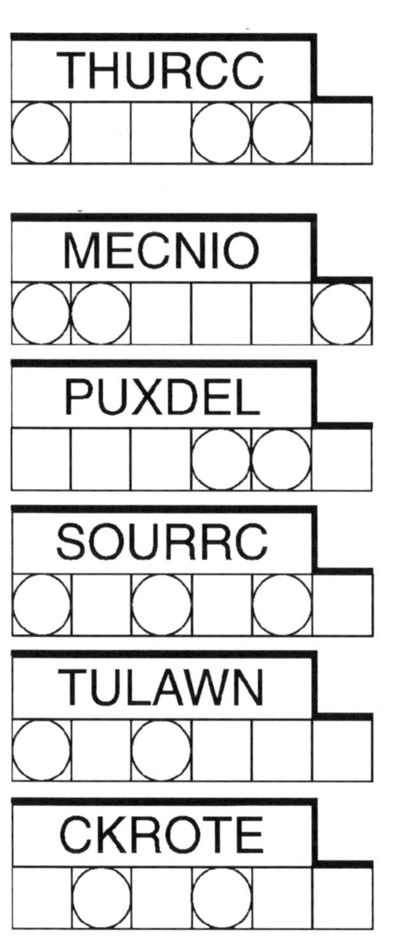
THURCC
MECNIO
PUXDEL
SOURRC
TULAWN
CKROTE

I bet these bring back memories!
I know every part of every car I salvaged.
HIS MEMORY OF THE HUGE AUTO SALVAGE YARD HE ONCE OWNED WAS A ---

Now arrange the circled letters to form the surprise answer, as suggested by the above cartoon.

Print answer here

JUMBLE®

Unscramble these six Jumbles, one letter to each square, to form six ordinary words.

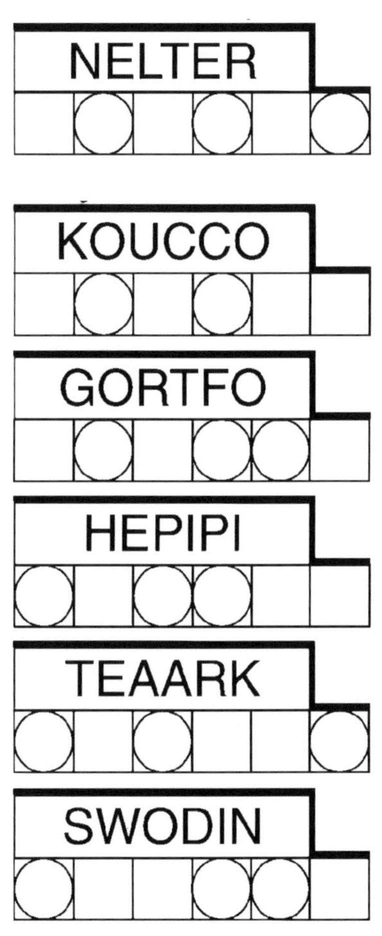
NELTER
KOUCCO
GORTFO
HEPIPI
TEAARK
SWODIN

Wow! Let's see how long it'll fly. I can't wait to see your next design.
I'm going to give it some more string.
WHEN SHE AND HER FATHER FLEW THE KITE SHE'D BUILT BY HAND, HE SAID ---

Now arrange the circled letters to form the surprise answer, as suggested by the above cartoon.

Print answer here

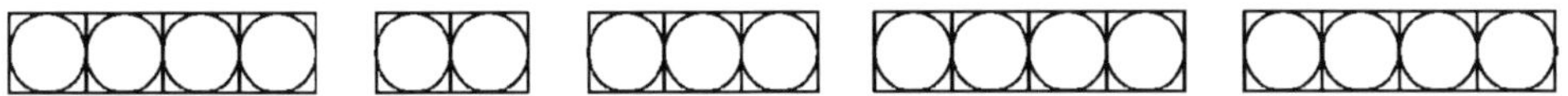

JUMBLE®

Unscramble these six Jumbles, one letter to each square, to form six ordinary words.

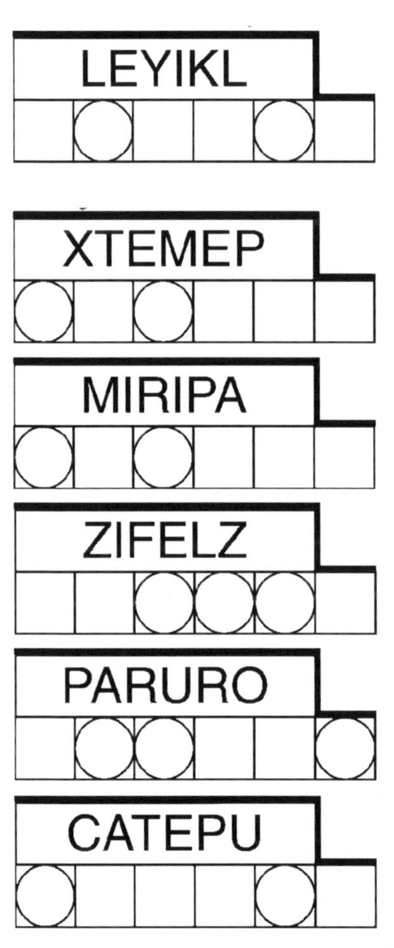
LEYIKL
XTEMEP
MIRIPA
ZIFELZ
PARURO
CATEPU

Let's go, Mike!
Associated Press Picnic
Let's win this for the Times!
On three!
Wow! They really want to win this.
They're going to yank their arms off.
THE WRITERS PLAYED TUG-O-WAR AT THEIR OUTING. THE WINNERS WOULD GET A ---

Now arrange the circled letters to form the surprise answer, as suggested by the above cartoon.

Print answer here

JUMBLE®

Unscramble these six Jumbles, one letter to each square, to form six ordinary words.

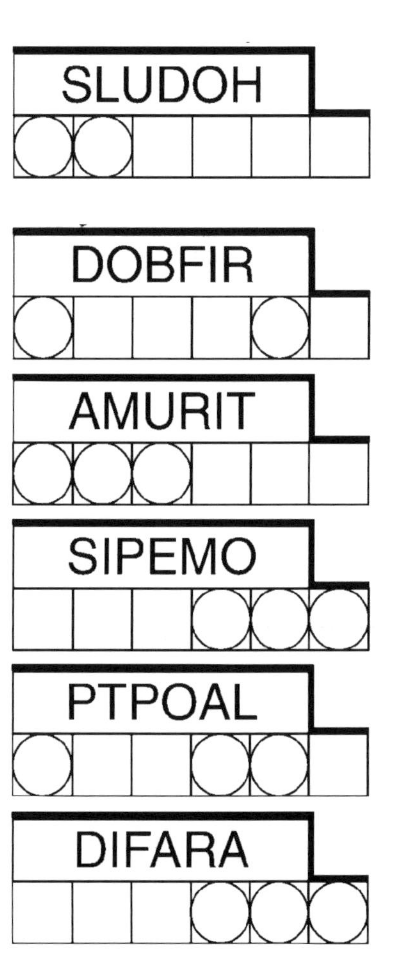
SLUDOH
DOBFIR
AMURIT
SIPEMO
PTPOAL
DIFARA

Is it a Spanish doubloon?
I can't tell!
Can I buy candy with it?
THE COIN WAS IN SUCH BAD CONDITION, THEY COULDN'T MAKE ---

Now arrange the circled letters to form the surprise answer, as suggested by the above cartoon.

Print answer here

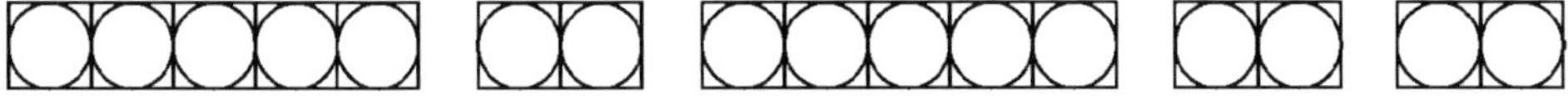

JUMBLE®

Unscramble these six Jumbles, one letter to each square, to form six ordinary words.

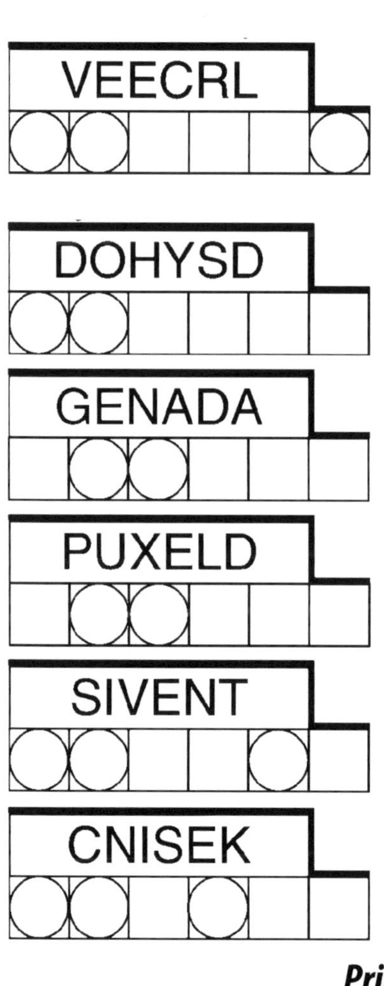
VEECRL
DOHYSD
GENADA
PUXELD
SIVENT
CNISEK

Maybe I should have had this professionally done. You missed a spot.
Maybe you should have!
WHEN HE COMPLAINED TO HIS WIFE ABOUT HOW SHE IRONED HIS SHIRT, HE WAS ---

Now arrange the circled letters to form the surprise answer, as suggested by the above cartoon.

Print answer here

JUMBLE®

Unscramble these six Jumbles, one letter to each square, to form six ordinary words.

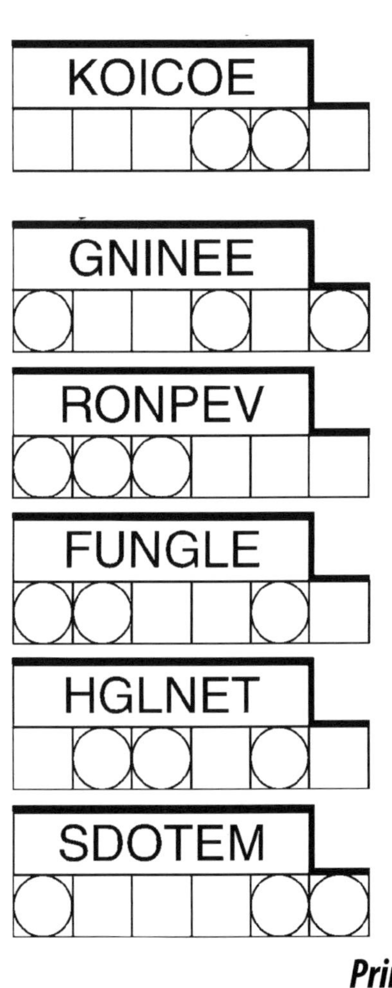
KOICOE
GNINEE
RONPEV
FUNGLE
HGLNET
SDOTEM

I'm finally ready to give this to you. I've been working on it for years. It's one of a kind and now, it's yours.
We've always wanted one. Now, we have it!
Now, this just made my day!
HE GAVE THEM THE HANDMADE CLOCK AT THAT MOMENT BECAUSE THERE WAS ---

Now arrange the circled letters to form the surprise answer, as suggested by the above cartoon.

Print answer here

THE

JUMBLE®

Unscramble these six Jumbles, one letter to each square, to form six ordinary words.

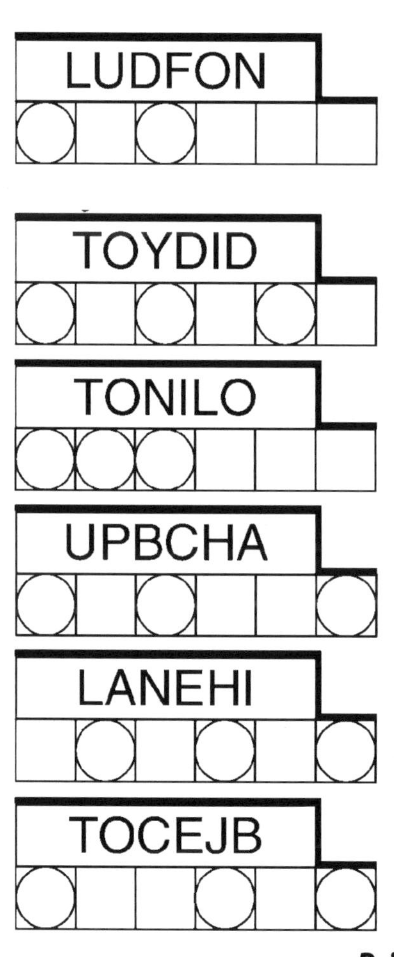
LUDFON
TOYDID
TONILO
UPBCHA
LANEHI
TOCEJB

It was a long day at the restaurants, but it pays the bills for now.
I'm glad you're home, Mom. What did you bring us for dinner?
SHE WORKED TWO WAITRESSING JOBS TO ---

Now arrange the circled letters to form the surprise answer, as suggested by the above cartoon.

Print answer here

Answers

1. **Jumbles:** MESSY COACH BUREAU MISERY
Answer: What the bridge on the violin enables the player to get—HIS MUSIC "ACROSS"
2. **Jumbles:** MADLY WEARY FIZZLE JINGLE
Answer: Formerly found only in the country but now commonly seen in the city—WILD LIFE
3. **Jumbles:** SLANT HUMAN VIOLIN WOEFUL
Answer: What the bigamist would like to keep—"TWO" HIMSELF
4. **Jumbles:** FOLIO VIGIL BOBBIN GROUCH
Answer: What were Alexander Graham Bell's first words?—GOO GOO
5. **Jumbles:** AWOKE MINOR DRUDGE PIGPEN
Answer: Another name for a philanderer—A DAME DROPPER
6. **Jumbles:** WEDGE BRAND LIKELY PEWTER
Answer: What the hypochondriac was sick of—BEING WELL
7. **Jumbles:** MOUND GUMBO MUTTON BYGONE
Answer: What somebody who tries to please everybody is apt to remain—A NOBODY
8. **Jumbles:** BARGE LEAFY TYRANT HOURLY
Answer: What they called her husband who was addicted to gambling—HER "BETTOR" HALF
9. **Jumbles:** CLEFT GUIDE DONKEY FLAXEN
Answer: A day off is sometimes followed by this—AN OFF DAY
10. **Jumbles:** LEAVE MAJOR CROUCH BUTTER
Answer: What the outlaws turned skydivers had—A "CHUTE" OUT
11. **Jumbles:** TOXIC YACHT HUNGRY CURFEW
Answer: What that road hog believes "might" makes—RIGHT—OF WAY
12. **Jumbles:** FOYER YEARN SYSTEM HEARTH
Answer: A person who always borrows trouble is usually anxious to do this—SHARE IT WITH OTHERS
13. **Jumbles:** MOURN UTTER LAYOFF POWDER
Answer: What yeast is—FLOUR POWER
14. **Jumbles:** LEGAL IRATE BRANDY RABBIT
Answer: Another name for sarcasm—BARBED "IRE"
15. **Jumbles:** WOMEN IDIOM GHETTO JOSTLE
Answer: He lies in wait for a fish, and after catching it he does this—LIES IN WEIGHT
16. **Jumbles:** FILMY CRESS OUTING THWART
Answer: On a blind date he was expecting a "vision," but it turned out to be this—A "SIGHT"
17. **Jumbles:** PIETY WAFER GOLFER THRIVE
Answer: What the bus driver told him—WHERE TO GET OFF
18. **Jumbles:** MIRTH ITCHY UPWARD HEARSE
Answer: One way to save face is to learn to keep this—PART OF IT SHUT
19. **Jumbles:** DERBY JOUST DAMASK POLLEN
Answer: A woman can say more in a look than a man can in this—A BOOK
20. **Jumbles:** GIANT AROMA CHORUS DILUTE
Answer: If a job is to have a future, it's likely to depend on this—THE MAN WHO HOLDS IT
21. **Jumbles:** FAINT PHOTO DREDGE STYLUS
Answer: A guy who's always boasting about his family tree probably comes from this—ITS SHADY SIDE
22. **Jumbles:** UNCLE LYING PRAYER INVEST
Answer: How the undertaker presented his bill—GRAVELY
23. **Jumbles:** FRAME HITCH BOUNCE ABUSED
Answer: She has what it takes to wear the latest fashions—A RICH HUSBAND
24. **Jumbles:** EATEN FENCE HINDER DETAIN
Answer: Goliath was surprised by what David did because such a thing had never this before—ENTERED HIS HEAD
25. **Jumbles:** BRAVE LOWLY GADFLY HUNTER
Answer: That windbag was always getting carried away by the sound of his own voice, but never this—FAR ENOUGH
26. **Jumbles:** TOOTH COUPE KILLER VANDAL
Answer: She was never overlooked but usually this—LOOKED OVER
27. **Jumbles:** OAKEN MERGE POSTAL NUMBER
Answer: A person who wakes up to find himself famous may not have this—BEEN ASLEEP
28. **Jumbles:** BATCH JOKER LIQUID PURVEY
Answer: When the kids have to play in on account of bad weather, the parents often end up this way—PLAYED OUT
29. **Jumbles:** FRAUD PATIO DAMPEN LOCALE
Answer: That visitor who drops in for a call might actually be wanting to do this—CALL IN FOR A DROP
30. **Jumbles:** DROOP LARVA SURELY CIPHER
Answer: What the intellectual hobo was—A ROAD SCHOLAR
31. **Jumbles:** TRILL DIZZY KIDNAP LATEST
Answer: What there was a lot of at the unemployment office—"IDLE" TALK
32. **Jumbles:** QUAKE TARDY MUSCLE PAGODA
Answer: A blaze can be very hot, especially when it's this—"COALED"
33. **Jumbles:** MONEY SOUSE VIRILE IMPUTE
Answer: The landlord's promises were no better than this—HIS PREMISES
34. **Jumbles:** JUICE MOUSY UNCLAD PONDER
Answer: How a guy usually finds himself when he's always asking around for a loan—ALONE
35. **Jumbles:** POPPY VIPER POTENT JANGLE
Answer: What a good memory requires—NO PEN OR PAPER
36. **Jumbles:** LIVEN BARON CROTCH EMBALM
Answer: What they called the rear entrance of that cafeteria—THE BACTERIA
37. **Jumbles:** ODIUM PANDA SKEWER DRAGON
Answer: How they felt when teacher gave a zero to everyone in the class—"DE-GRADED"
38. **Jumbles:** RAPID FEVER HOOKUP NUTRIA
Answer: What the loafer's life work was—TO AVOID IT
39. **Jumbles:** THINK CRANK POMADE ICEBOX
Answer: What safe driving is—NO ACCIDENT
40. **Jumbles:** SUAVE AWARD JUMBLE UNLOCK
Answer: For an opinion to be sound it must not be this—ALL SOUND
41. **Jumbles:** BERTH ENSUE UPKEEP VELVET
Answer: What his wife's little poodle was—HIS PET PEEVE
42. **Jumbles:** TRUTH WHISK KOSHER YEARLY
Answer: What the "wino" said when offered a little sip—"WHY, YES"
43. **Jumbles:** PARCH WHILE KITTEN HICCUP
Answer: What a marriage proposal is—A HITCH PITCH
44. **Jumbles:** JOLLY ARBOR SUBTLY LOTION
Answer: How "sharp" remarks may be expressed, oddly enough—BLUNTLY
45. **Jumbles:** CHOKE PARTY FUTURE LIMPID
Answer: America's most outstanding public figure—THE DEFICIT
46. **Jumbles:** PIKER LITHE DROPSY SAVAGE
Answer: A poet who hopes to make his living from writing verses is apt to experience many of these—REVERSES

47. Jumbles: TWEAK BEIGE EMBODY FRACAS
Answer: Why those other doctors resented the orthopedist—HE GOT ALL THE BREAKS

48. Jumbles: NUDGE INLET GRASSY UPHELD
Answer: A nuclear physicist is another man whose wife doesn't this—UNDERSTAND HIM

49. Jumbles: AISLE CHAIR INLAND HOMAGE
Answer: What the phrenologist was—HEAD MAN

50. Jumbles: JINGO SHEAF PILFER MUSEUM
Answer: What the heroic fireman became—"FLAM-OUS"

51. Jumbles: BUMPY MOGUL WHENCE FALLEN
Answer: What they thought when he rounded second base—THERE'S NO PLACE LIKE HOME

52. Jumbles: STOKE FETID ADRIFT MASCOT
Answer: People who love shellfish become hungry when they do this—" SEA" FOOD

53. Jumbles: BASSO PRIME JOVIAL COUPON
Answer: What the cattle tycoon made a lot of—"MOO-LA"

54. Jumbles: GLAND AWASH BANTER GUITAR
Answer: How the winner was chosen at that big art contest—BY A DRAWING

55. Jumbles: MOCHA LANKY DETACH TUMULT
Answer: What a climb up that little hill didn't do—"A-MOUNT" TO MUCH

56. Jumbles: BROOD TWICE GLANCE DISMAL
Answer: What the saleslady said when asked whether that new type foundation garment is really going to work—"OF CORS-ET" WILL

57. Jumbles: CHAMP JUMPY MUSTER BUNKER
Answer: What she does when she kisses her hockey player boyfriend—"PUCK-ERS" UP

58. Jumbles: TWILL DUCHY FAMOUS APPEAR
Answer: What happened when the safety match tycoon lots his temper—HE FLARED UP

59. Jumbles: MIDGE TUNED HEALTH IMPUGN
Answer: Why the flower vendor was arrested—FOR "PETAL-ING"

60. Jumbles: EIGHT SNORT BOUGHT EXOTIC
Answer: When his tongue is loose, it's often because he is this—"TIGHT"

61. Jumbles: KNEEL HANDY MYSELF PIRATE
Answer: What those corduroy pillows made—HEAD LINES

62. Jumbles: WHOOP BORAX INJECT HAMMER
Answer: What kind of a problem did the captain face?—A "MAJOR" ONE

63. Jumbles: UNIFY OBESE GAIETY ASYLUM
Answer: Why the carpenter needed all that emergency dental work—HE BIT HIS NAILS

64. Jumbles: NAÏVE OUTDO FORAGE ADMIRE
Answer: What your telephone might become if you fail to pay the bill—A DEAD RINGER

65. Jumbles: SYNOD ABHOR FORKED TACKLE
Answer: Why the employee at the car factory was fired—HE TOOK A "BRAKE"

66. Jumbles: TYPED LUNGE BUCKET ACCENT
Answer: He went to the shrink for a checkup for this—THE NECK UP

67. Jumbles: VIRUS BOOTY PLAGUE AFLOAT
Answer: The baker hired—and then fired—A "LOAF-ER"

68. Jumbles: MANGE WHOSE INDUCT EXODUS
Answer: For not shoveling the sidewalk there—SNOW EXCUSE

69. Jumbles: RANCH PORGY DENTAL JACKET
Answer: What some not-so-young actors find it difficult to do—ACT THEIR AGE

70. Jumbles: PLAIT HENCE NOTIFY MAINLY
Answer: What they called the guy who was nuts about fishing—A "FINN-ATIC"

71. Jumbles: TULLE QUASH GUIDED PUDDLE
Answer: What happened after he bought a new pair of suspenders?—HE WAS HELD UP

72. Jumbles: TRAIT POKED MEMOIR CONCUR
Answer: What the dropout from the data processing school must have been—A "NIN-COMPUTER"

73. Jumbles: RAJAH MURKY CATCHY HAIRDO
Answer: In those years straw hats had this—THEIR "HAY" DAY

74. Jumbles: YOKEL WAGON BAFFLE GRIMLY
Answer: What that golf nut had in his eyes—A "FAIR-WAY" LOOK

75. Jumbles: FORGO SIEGE ALWAYS INVOKE
Answer: When they film a wintry scene in Hollywood, the prop man has to come up with plenty of these—SNOW FAKES

76. Jumbles: JOINT VALVE MUSKET HARBOR
Answer: I've finally bought you a watch for your birthday, dear—"IT'S ABOUT TIME"

77. Jumbles: BEGOT FORAY HAPPEN PARISH
Answer: The only thing that children wear out faster than shoes—PARENTS

78. Jumbles: AGENT HOUSE FONDLY TOFFEE
Answer: How the traffic cop's girlfriend caught him—FLAT-FOOTED

79. Jumbles: JADED TANGY BRONCO INVADE
Answer: The media thought they'd better give the event plenty of this—"COVERAGE"

80. Jumbles: QUEST DUMPY INFECT FROTHY
Answer: What the karate champ turned restaurant owner specialized in—CHOPS

81. Jumbles: TRIPE FISHY SINFUL INVITE
Answer: How they celebrated the new year at that old-time saloon—WITH "FIST-IVITIES"

82. Jumbles: ERUPT YOUNG GUNNER REALTY
Answer: "A man sold me the Nile River for ten dollars."—"E-GYPT" YOU (he gypped you)

83. Jumbles: FIFTY RIGOR MYRIAD INLAID
Answer: Somebody who calls a spade a spade might want to give you this—A DIRTY "DIG"

84. Jumbles: SAVOR FAIRY RADIUM HALLOW
Answer: A live wire is never backward in going there —FORWARD

85. Jumbles: QUEUE BERET GOPHER DEMISE
Answer: What the rope tycoon built—A HUGE "HEMP-IRE"

86. Jumbles: DRAMA TEPID CIRCUS NOVICE
Answer: What you should get before investing in expensive audio equipment—"SOUND" ADVICE

87. Jumbles: BLOOD SHAKY CAVORT GLOOMY
Answer: He won the biggest bet at the greyhound race because he had this—A "HOT" DOG

88. Jumbles: AZURE SWAMP FEUDAL CANOPY
Answer: What many a public speaker devotes his life to—A "WORDY" CAUSE

89. Jumbles: RODEO GUARD FALTER NUANCE
Answer: The bachelor thought he'd purchase some acreage while he was still this—"UN-LANDED"

90. Jumbles: FEINT ANNOY HIDING EXEMPT
Answer: What bitter cold weather sometimes is—NEXT TO "NOTHING"

91. Jumbles: COMET KNIFE JUNIOR QUARTZ
Answer: A guy should be this when he goes on a diet—QUIET

92. Jumbles: TRACT ACRID CONVEX BUBBLE
Answer: What the India rubber man at the circus got—BOUNCED

93. Jumbles: CRUSH MADAM COERCE PICNIC
Answer: A miser lives poor so he can do this—DIE RICH

94. Jumbles: FOIST BIRCH SALOON ASSURE
Answer: These words sometimes describe a lawsuit—A LOSS SUIT

95. **Jumbles:** ENEMY DOUBT TRYING SUNDAE
Answer: What a guy who pays to enter the marathon is sure to get—A RUN FOR HIS MONEY

96. **Jumbles:** FAUNA HEAVY MEMORY AUTUMN
Answer: Pollution is the contamination of nature by this—HUMAN NATURE

97. **Jumbles:** LOONY BRAIN SMUDGE COSTLY
Answer: Where you might find those optometry students—IN THE "GLASS" ROOM

98. **Jumbles:** JUDGE FLOOD ARCADE OVERDO
Answer: Appropriate for the guy who wins the cowboy-father-of-the-year award—A "DUDE-DAD"

99. **Jumbles:** CHAFE DRONE WISDOM RARITY
Answer: He's sometimes weather-wise, but more often this—OTHERWISE

100. **Jumbles:** MERCY GUILT DUPLEX SNUGLY
Answer: What the first dentist to open an office in the Old West was called—THE "GUM-SLINGER"

101. **Jumbles:** ORBIT SOUPY HIATUS SAYING
Answer: They loved the new wine bar and its—BIG "POUR-TIONS"

102. **Jumbles:** PARTY FLING MOTIVE HERBAL
Answer: Big Ben may be the most famous clock—OF ALL TIME

103. **Jumbles:** CONGA PANTS STEREO HECTIC
Answer: The landlord wouldn't sign for tenants' packages,—NO "ACCEPTIONS"

104. **Jumbles:** ICIER JOKER DAMAGE SECOND
Answer: Deciding what to study in college can be a—MAJOR DECISION

105. **Jumbles:** TRULY TIPSY FRIGID LOUDLY
Answer: The owner of the maid service was making a—TIDY PROFIT

106. **Jumbles:** UTTER ENACT HAIRDO CURFEW
Answer: "Star Trek" was canceled after three seasons, but its success was set—IN THE FUTURE

107. **Jumbles:** AWAIT VENOM CREAMY HARDER
Answer: When the penguin left to hang out with his buddies, his wife said—HAVE AN "ICE" DAY

108. **Jumbles:** MODEM TARDY IMPOSE GARAGE
Answer: Maybe the reason some people watch too much TV is that they are—PROGRAMMED TO

109. **Jumbles:** CURVE MOOSE DEFACE GLASSY
Answer: Crime was on the rise and some people were becoming—ALARMED

110. **Jumbles:** GRIME ABOUT TIGHTS DRENCH
Answer: When they found listening devices in their office—IT BUGGED THEM

111. **Jumbles:** ENJOY TEASE INCOME TANGLE
Answer: When the pirate saw the treasure wasn't where the map said, he—LOST IT

112. **Jumbles:** HEDGE HITCH GLITCH NOTION
Answer: Porky Pig's success made it possible for him to live—HIGH ON THE HOG

113. **Jumbles:** ITCHY GOING NEPHEW SCROLL
Answer: When the pharaoh employed an artist to decorate his tomb, it was a case of—"HIRE-O-GLYPHICS"

114. **Jumbles:** WHISK THIRD CANVAS BOUNTY
Answer: The fishermen paid for large minnows, but it looked like it was a—BAIT AND SWITCH

115. **Jumbles:** STOMP PAUSE SKIMPY EQUATE
Answer: When Mickey needed to sneak back into the house, he was—QUIET AS A MOUSE

116. **Jumbles:** YOUNG WEDGE SAFETY JAGUAR
Answer: When the twins ordered the "Buy One, Get One Free" lunch special, it was—"TWOS-DAY"

117. **Jumbles:** EPOXY BUSHY MOTION NEEDLE
Answer: The prizefighter needed to get his possessions ready to be moved, so he—BOXED THEM UP

118. **Jumbles:** WEAVE FRAME METRIC INFECT
Answer: When asked if they had mattresses that weren't so soft, the salesman said—AFFIRMATIVE

119. **Jumbles:** TIGER BROOD MAGNET CHANGE
Answer: The battle between Sleepy Hollow's horsemen was—COMING TO A HEAD

120. **Jumbles:** RURAL ANNOY MERELY COMMON
Answer: After putting sesame seeds on hamburger buns, his business was—ON A ROLL

121. **Jumbles:** PATIO YOUTH GOSSIP PASTRY
Answer: After getting stuck in a middle seat at 30,000 feet, she was—UPTIGHT

122. **Jumbles:** PRONG TARDY EXTENT FOSSIL
Answer: To destroy the town and get home for dinner, Godzilla had to—STEP ON IT

123. **Jumbles:** TROLL QUILT FAIRLY ALLEGE
Answer: When he said the U.S. produces 200 million tons of trash annually, he meant it—"LITTER-ALLY"

124. **Jumbles:** DRESS AFOOT SAILOR MAGPIE
Answer: When asked if the horror film was too scary for his little brother, he said—I'M AFRAID SO

125. **Jumbles:** AGILE DROOP SYMBOL HONCHO
Answer: The popular choir was paid to perform around the world and made—GOOD "HAR-MONEY"

126. **Jumbles:** SPOIL ERUPT PROVEN SYSTEM
Answer: Her students were beginning to understand addition and subtraction—MORE OR LESS

127. **Jumbles:** COUGH DRANK WINERY SNAPPY
Answer: The mallards were ready to cross the road, now that they had their—DUCKS IN A ROW

128. **Jumbles:** FAINT TRULY DRENCH DREAMY
Answer: The first baseball gloves were—HAND-CRAFTED

129. **Jumbles:** PRONG FUNNY UNDONE PODIUM
Answer: Though smaller, the carpenter was better than his larger co-worker—POUND FOR POUND

130. **Jumbles:** RAZOR LOUSY FLURRY POETIC
Answer: Compared to Hubble, the James Webb Space Telescope will be—FAR SUPERIOR

131. **Jumbles:** OCCUR CABIN PLURAL WEAKLY
Answer: The tiger leapt at his prey, but he missed. He was bummed, but he'd—"POUNCE" BACK

132. **Jumbles:** TREND AWAIT BOTHER SUBMIT
Answer: The author loved working in her basement office where she felt—"WRITE" AT HOME

133. **Jumbles:** TASTY MESSY SWAMPY ACCEPT
Answer: When the police station became infested with flies, they brought in a—SWAT TEAM

134. **Jumbles:** VOICE TULIP BROKEN BISECT
Answer: When asked what your blood type is, sometimes you need to—BE POSITIVE

135. **Jumbles:** BANJO PHONY EYELID HYBRID
Answer: The actress was excited to get the part in the play. She was finally on the—"PAY-ROLE"

136. **Jumbles:** BIKER HANDY LUCENT PENCIL
Answer: She asked the obnoxious vampire to leave her alone when he became a—PAIN IN THE NECK

137. **Jumbles:** CURLY TOPAZ SANDAL COPPER
Answer: To get to the summit of Mount Everest, climbers have to—PAY TOP DOLLAR

138. **Jumbles:** TRACT ENJOY EYEFUL SAVORY
Answer: The best student in the speed-reading class was a—FAST LEARNER